D0837503

Need more help?
Email me!

I can help!

This process doesn't need to be hard! I am available to help you get your best LSAT score and best law school admissions offers. I love this stuff and know a lot about it, so reach out with any questions you have. You can reach me at **ben@lsasimplified.com**. You can also check out my current offerings at lsasimplified.com.

You can also find me on Instagram where I post about upcoming LSATs, general LSAT news, and tips regarding this process. I offer live courses over Zoom as well as private tutoring for anyone that wants to work with me face to face.

 LSA Simplified

LSA Simplified's LSAT Primer

By Ben Parker

Table of Contents

Prologue

Welcome. I'm Ben, and in these following hundred pages, I will teach you a simple and effective way to prepare for the LSAT.

Preparing to take the LSAT can be daunting. A whole industry exists to convince you that this test is complicated. I don't believe them. The LSAT doesn't have to be complicated. My goal in this book is to convince you that the LSAT is an easy and simple test if you approach it correctly. Does that mean you can read this book and score a 180 right away? No. It will take work. But, if you do the work correctly and give it time, you will score well.

My LSAT methodology is simple. Make the LSAT simple. You just need to understand the words on the page. That's right! There are no gimmicks or tricks that you need to know to do well on the LSAT. You do not need to learn how to diagram arguments or learn any new vocabulary words from a textbook. You just need to get really good at understanding what is written on the page. If you know what is going on, you will score high. I wholeheartedly believe that this is the best way to tackle the LSAT. I won't talk about analytics, LSAT jargon, or formal logic. All those things hurt my head, and more importantly, they are unnecessary. These "LSAT tips" made me worse at the test when I studied. In fact, I got into the 170s when I threw out all the LSAT jargon and just focused on the words on the page.

Funnily enough, this "simple approach" sets me apart from many other folks in the LSAT prep industry. Other prep programs often have acronyms for what you should be focusing on. I have an acronym for you: UTDWOTP (you don't have to remember this).

Understand the damn words on the page.

That's the LSAT tip that will help you get to where you want to be. If you commit to understanding every single word the LSAT says, the sky's the limit. If you think that's too hard, I have to ask if you're going into the right field. Lawyers do not gimmick their way through motions or briefs, so why should we on the LSAT?

The LSAT becomes a game if you commit to understanding the test. You get to point out the holes in the test's bullshit arguments. For all of you who want to go to law school because "you are good at arguing," the LSAT is a test to see if that is true. Commit to learning this test; not only will your law school offers be better, but you will also be positioned to be a better lawyer. The dirty little secret of LSAT prep is that some of this stuff just isn't that hard. So commit to understanding the test, and you will be doing the LSAT the easy way.

That being said, if you get through this book and you'd rather diagram out arguments and study for 8 hours a day, be my guest. But, in these next 100 pages, I am confident I will show you the easy way to approach this test.

This book won't get you from 135-175, but it will lay the groundwork for you to self-study efficiently. It will teach you how to approach this test. I cannot do the work for you, but I can be a guide so that you are not flailing around trying to prepare. I'll show you the road you must take; it's just up to you if you're willing to do the work.

Introduction to the LSAT

What is the LSAT?

Alright, so you've made it through my prologue, and you are ready to give this a shot, but now you might ask yourself, "What even is the LSAT?"

The LSAT is a test the ABA (American Bar Association) requires for law school admissions. It is similar to the SAT or ACT in that it tests skills that measure your ability to perform in school. Specifically, the LSAT tests how well you can read, how well you understand logic, and how well you can get through the logic puzzles known as logic games. These logic puzzles test your ability to see how different conditions interact.

The LSAT is composed of three scored multiple-choice sections (logical reasoning (LR), reading comprehension (RC), and logic games (LG)). You have 35 minutes per section. There is also one random section thrown at you on test day. This section is the experimental section. The experimental section is one of the three scored sections (so a random LR, LG, or RC section), but it will not be scored. Don't even worry about this because there is nothing you can do to control which section is experimental. On test day, you will just be taking four sections and must perform well on all four.

Some may think this is a stupid test that is just a hurdle you have to get through. If you believe this, you are wrong. The LSAT ultimately tests two critical skills for law students and lawyers.

1. How good are you at understanding English and logic
2. How hard can you work

Lawyers fight each other using words as weapons. You need to know what words mean, what is logically sound, and what is not so that you can be a good lawyer. If you are in court and opposing counsel is making some BS argument, you need to be able to object and point out what they are doing wrong. These skills are what LR tests.

In law school, you will have to read long cases. Not only do you have to read these cases, but you must also understand what they are saying. Simply skimming your eyes across the pages is not going to cut it. You have to make sure you *comprehend* what you are reading. These skills are what RC tests.

LG is a little sneakier in what it tests. It tests how conditions interact, but what it really tests is how hard you are willing to work. Nobody sits down and kills the games. Nearly everyone scores terribly the first time they sit down with this section. So how does this apply to legal practice? Well, lawyers and law students work hard to master things. LG tests whether you are willing to grind through a complex topic to master it. If you don't have the chops to do this on LG for the LSAT, why would you be able to do this later in your career? LG tests if you have the necessary work ethic to be a lawyer.

Is this test perfect? No. But it is the most predictive measure of law school success, so commit to doing well on it. Even if you think it's dumb, you still need to do well on it if you are serious about being a lawyer. After all, it controls your admissions chances.

Why does the LSAT Matter?

Put simply, the LSAT is the most important part of your application. The first thing that law schools do when they receive your application is perform an index calculation. This index calculation follows some version of this formula.

LSAT*constant + Undergrad GPA*constant = Index number

As you can see, your index number is a product of only two numbers. At most law schools, the LSAT counts much more than GPA. Some schools, such as UC Berkeley, emphasize GPA. However, even at Berkeley, they care about your LSAT. Put simply, the LSAT is the most essential part of your application.

These index numbers allow law schools to consolidate both of your numbers into one workable number so they can rank all their incoming applications. This calculation enables them to save time. If you have low enough numbers, Harvard Law will not admit you. Similarly, lower-ranked schools are forced to consider your application if you have high enough numbers.

Law schools will put your application into one of three piles based on your index number. Presumptive admit (applications that are likely to get in), presumptive deny (applications that are unlikely to get in), and committee (applications they review in-depth because they are on the margins). Your law school options have already been determined based on your GPA and LSAT score.

Not only does LSAT determine where you get in, but it also determines how much scholarship money you will get. Your numbers almost entirely determine scholarship money in law school.

Why does your LSAT score decide scholarship money? Schools use scholarship money to bid on high-quality candidates. When I say high-quality candidates, I mean candidates that will raise their ranking. Their rankings are affected by many factors, but the only factors in your application that go into the school's ranking are your undergraduate GPA and LSAT score. They care about raising (or keeping) their ranking, so they prioritize high numbers. Even if you connect with an admissions dean personally, you might still get denied if accepting you would lower their ranking.

You need to understand that the LSAT is the most crucial aspect of your law school application. Nobody's personal statement overcomes an LSAT deficiency. Your GPA is likely already set (if it's not, ensure you are getting As). The best thing you can do to get good admission offers is to get a high LSAT.

Simplify the LSAT

My trade name for LSAT prep is LSA Simplified. LSA stands for "law school admissions," but I heavily focus on the LSAT. I have found that simplifying the LSAT is the best way to approach it.

I don't have many LSAT "tricks" that I will impart to you in this book. Instead, I will provide a guide to doing questions so that you can see the right thought processes to do well on this test. It won't involve learning all sorts of "strategies." Instead, we will focus on being critical of arguments and committing to understanding every word on the page.

This test makes sense. If you understand it, you will do excellent.

How to Study for the LSAT

The bulk of your LSAT study needs to be done by actually doing questions. If you have not taken a diagnostic yet, set this book down, take one, and come back to this book after you have completed a full LSAT under timed conditions. You can find a free PDF of the June 2007 LSAT by googling June 2007 LSAT, or you can sign up for Lawhub which has access to 70+ old LSATs. You should purchase this anyways, so you may as well get it now.

Once you have finished this book, you should get on a self-study schedule of doing roughly a section a day. Do the section under timed conditions and thoroughly reviewed your mistakes once you have completed each section. Now, even though the timer is on, you should not be rushing. The point of having the timer on is so that you learn to disregard it.

Most people should not be finishing sections in the allotted 35 minutes. The key to getting good at the LSAT is to go slow but have very high accuracy on the questions you are doing. By practicing this way, you will understand more and make it further in the sections. I would rather you get 10/10 questions right on a section and have to guess on the remaining 15 than score 12/25 but have attempted every question. The person who got 10/10 is much easier to teach because they do not allow themselves to make dumb mistakes. The person scoring 12/25 is making mistakes. Now, this doesn't mean that you will have 100% accuracy, but you need to hold yourself to a high standard. You have to build the understanding first, and once you create understanding, speed will come.

Each day you should be doing a section. In this book, you will learn in detail about the three different sections and how to approach them with accuracy. Once you have built the accuracy, speed will come.

After you finish your section, you need to review your mistakes. For any question you did and got wrong, you need to dive into that question and figure out what you misunderstood.

Ask yourself the following questions
1. Why did I pick the wrong answer?
2. What did I miss about the correct answer?
3. How am I going to avoid those mistakes in the future?

If you do this consistently, you will make progress. The LSAT will tell you what you don't understand through the questions you miss. By studying this way, you can fill in those gaps in your knowledge. Once you've filled your gaps, you will score high! It really is that simple. I'll have a more in-depth study schedule at the end of the book.

LSAT Myths

Before we get into the nitty-gritty of actual questions, I wanted to address some of the most common LSAT myths.

Myth 1: You can only improve 10-15 points on the LSAT.
Fact: This is nonsense. People can go up tons of points and do it all the time. I regularly see people I work with go up 20 points. I've even seen improvements of 30+ points. The only limitations on your LSAT score are the ones you impose upon yourself.

Myth 2: You should study untimed.
Fact: You can study untimed, but it removes one of the main difficulties of the LSAT, which is the time pressure you have to take it under on test day. Many people refuse to do timed practice and then crash and burn on test day. Study timed so that you get used to the clock. If you study under gameday conditions, gameday is not stressful. Even if you study untimed, you still need to study timed. So, simplify the whole process and time your sections instead of planning out which days are untimed and timed. Please don't rush to complete them, but get used to the clock. The whole point of having the timer on while you take the test is to get accustomed to ignoring it. The only thing I want you to focus on during a section is getting the question you're on correct.

Myth 3: Formal logic helps on the LSAT.
Fact: No, it doesn't. Sure, you can diagram arguments, but you do not need to. Many students from other prep programs push back on this since it is so emphasized, but I never learned how to diagram statements such as "all foxes are red." We don't have to write something like "If F → Red." I trust that you are intelligent enough to understand that "all foxes are red" conceptually. It's not that hard. Diagramming overcomplicates this test, takes up valuable time, and is unnecessary. If you still don't believe me, read through how I go through LR later in this book, and I am confident I can convince you that my way is superior.

Myth 4: You should only take the LSAT one time.

Fact: Law schools in the US only care about your highest score. Lower scores don't go into your index calculation, so they do not care. Now, if you jump from a 135 to a 175 on actual LSATs (and so law schools know about this), you should write an addendum explaining your jump. Other than that, they will not care about your jump from 155 to 162. Take it as many times as possible to get your highest possible score. You can take it three times per cycle or five times in five years.

Basic Logical Reasoning Concepts

Introduction to Logical Reasoning

Logical reasoning is the LSAT section that evaluates how well you can assess arguments. In this section, the LSAT will give you a set of statements. This set of statements will typically be in the form of an argument. The LSAT will then ask you a question about those statements. These questions often involve making the argument better or worse or pointing out a flaw. They might also ask you what we can conclude based on this argument or what a specific part of it is doing.

Your approach for LR questions should be to read the argument and attack it. You want to treat every argument as if you are opposing counsel in court. You should be coming up with objections and pushback against what the argument is saying. If the argument is logically sound, you should be surprised. Let's do an example so that you can see what I mean by this.

Read this argument and see what your reaction to it is. Remember, we want to point out *why* the speaker is wrong. We should be surprised if we do not have an objection to their argument. Read this yourself. Notice how you respond to it and if you have any objections to the argument.

PT20 Section 2 Question 10

Premiums for automobile accident insurance are often higher for red cars than for cars of other colors. To justify these higher charges, insurance companies claim that, overall, a greater percentage of red cars are involved in accidents than are cars of any other color. If this claim is true, then lives could undoubtedly be saved by banning red cars from the roads altogether.

Hopefully, you read this critically and had an objection to the reasoning of the speaker. If you didn't, that's fine. It just means that this question is a chance for you to learn something.

Let's analyze this argument together to see what our speaker does.

First, they say, "Premiums for automobile accident insurance are often higher for red cars than for cars of other colors." This sentence is a fact, and we cannot argue with it. However, we should still react. Why do red cars have a higher premium? Do people that drive red cars drive more dangerously? Is it possible that teenage boys, the most dangerous drivers on the road, make up a high proportion of red-car drivers? Do auto insurance companies just discriminate based on color preference?

Now, none of these possible reasons have to be true. The important part is that we are reacting. If you are reacting to what you are reading, it means you are understanding.

The author then says, "To justify these higher charges, insurance companies claim that, overall, a greater percentage of red cars are involved in accidents than are cars of any other color."

This is one of the possible thoughts we had to explain the first fact. If it is true that red cars crash more, it will make sense for insurance companies to charge more to insure cars. The insurance companies are just trying to have the premiums match the risk. However, we should note that the author says "claim," so the insurance companies may be lying. Maybe they discriminate based on car color, but I am inclined to agree that the real reason they charge red cars more is the higher likelihood of a crash.

The final sentence is, "If this claim is true, then lives could undoubtedly be saved by banning red cars from the roads altogether." This sentence is their conclusion, and it's where we want to call bullshit on them. We have made a considerable jump from our premises to our conclusion here. We know that red car drivers are more dangerous, but does that mean that banning red cars from the road will save lives? No, of course not. The red cars are dangerous because of the drivers, and if red cars are banned, we should expect those drivers to drive different cars. They could still drive dangerously in a black/white/blue/etc car, so the real problem is the drivers, not the cars. Therefore, banning red cars would not do anything except reduce the number of red cars on the road.

We've spotted a huge flaw, and the question is asking us to identify the flaw. The question is

---

The reasoning in the argument is flawed because

We have already identified the flaw, so we just need to find the same flaw in our answers. We are looking for an answer that says something like "dangerous drivers choose red cars disproportionately."

The answers are
   A. Accepts without question that insurance companies have the right to charge higher premiums for higher-risk clients
   B. Fails to consider whether red cars cost the same to repair as cars of other colors
   C. Ignores the possibility that drivers who drive recklessly have a preference for red cars
   D. Does not specify precisely what percentage of red cars are involved in accidents
   E. Makes an unsupported assumption that every automobile accident results in some loss of life

Only one of these answers correctly describes what we have identified, and several others are flat-out irrelevant. Let's go through them one by one.

A is talking about whether it is morally ok for insurance companies to charge more to high-risk clients. We do not care about what is ethically correct here. What we care about is "if we get rid of red cars on the road, will traffic accidents go down?" The argument concludes that banning cars will save lives. This answer is not addressing that point. Therefore, A is wrong.

B is talking about how much it costs to repair red cars. We don't care about maintenance costs. We care about "if we get rid of red cars, will that reduce traffic accidents?" Once again, B has nothing to do with the conclusion and is, therefore, wrong.

C is a great answer. It's telling us that reckless drivers choose red cars. If dangerous drivers choose red cars and those cars are banned, the dangerous drivers will choose other cars. Banning red cars will not solve the problem of unsafe drivers on the road. This flaw is what we spotted as we read the argument and will be the correct answer.

D is talking about what amount of red cars are in accidents. We do not care whether it is 100% or 1%. We care if banning red cars will reduce the amount. D does not point out the argument's flaw, so it is wrong.

E is just straight-up misdescribing the argument. In a flaw question, the answers have to reflect what the argument did, and the author never assumed that all car crashes result in a loss of life.

Hopefully, that felt easy. The LSAT is easy if you approach it by trying to understand what the test is doing.

Necessary and Sufficient

On the LSAT, you will run into necessary and sufficient conditions. While these words may seem arbitrary and confusing, the actual concepts they represent are simple.

When something is necessary, we need it to get a particular outcome. For example, it is necessary that we have water on a planet for there to be life. We know that if we have no water, there is no way that life will form. However, we also know that water does not guarantee life. Just because we found water on Planet X does not mean there will also be life there. Perhaps there is water, which is one necessary ingredient, but the planet is 300 degrees Fahrenheit. Even though we have water, we won't necessarily have life. This makes water a necessary condition.

A sufficient condition guarantees an outcome. An example of a sufficient condition is getting a piano dropped on your head. You will die if you get a grand piano dropped on your head. The piano being dropped on a person is sufficient for death. However, we know that a grand piano is not necessary for death. Someone could die in countless ways. For example, someone could have a heart attack, cancer, or be shot. Here, the piano being dropped on your head is a sufficient condition for death, but it is not necessary.

The LSAT will test you on every LR section to ensure you understand the difference between these two concepts. I'll give you an obvious one so you can object to my reasoning.

Everyone that gets shot with a cannon will die. Bob is dead. Therefore, Bob has been shot by a cannon.

You should have a pretty significant reaction to this. As we just talked about, there are countless ways that someone could die. Sure, a cannon causes death, but maybe Bob got run over by a semi-truck. Here, the argument confuses a sufficient condition (being shot with a cannon) with a necessary condition. If this were a flaw question, the correct answer would say something like "confuses a sufficient condition for a necessary condition."

People get confused by the jargon, but if you understand the underlying terms and what they mean, this is a pretty obvious flaw. They can also, and do, make this flaw going the other way. Let's take a look at what this looks like.

To make a cake, we need to have eggs in the recipe. This recipe calls for eggs. Therefore, this recipe must be for a cake.

In this argument, we are now confusing a necessary condition for a sufficient condition. We know that cakes need eggs in the recipe, but having eggs is not sufficient to make the recipe a cake recipe. This recipe could be for something else with eggs, such as an omelet.

These flaws should jump out to you as you read this section, and you should be able to spot them as you read the arguments in LR. Remember, your job in LR is to argue back, and if the author makes such a glaring hole, you need to point it out. These questions are free points if you spot this idea, so make sure you understand what these words mean in the abstract and how you can apply it to the question in front of you.

Correlation and Causation

Another common thing the LSAT does is confuse correlation and causation. You may be familiar with this flaw from past academic or life experiences. Still, I'll give you a quick rundown.

The LSAT will establish a correlation. Based on that correlation, the LSAT will conclude that one of the variables causes the other. Perhaps it is true that one variable causes the other, but we do not know that for sure based on only a correlation. Sometimes, there is causation, but it's the reverse of what they claim. They could make an argument like this:

Smoking and lung disease are correlated. Therefore, getting diagnosed with lung disease causes people to smoke.

Here, we should know from outside information that smoking and lung disease are correlated. But this is because smoking causes lung disease, and we make the reverse claim in this example argument. We say that lung disease causes smoking, which is silly. This is reverse causation and something the LSAT will often do.

The LSAT can also try to point out correlations where there are none. Take a look at this chart.

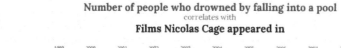

Number of people who drowned by falling into a pool
correlates with
Films Nicolas Cage appeared in

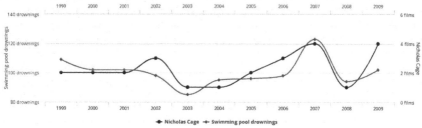

Here, we can see that the number of pool drownings correlates with Nicolas Cage appearing in films. The LSAT might make the following argument.

The amount of Nicolas Cage movies that come out per year correlates strongly with swimming pool drownings. Therefore, Nicolas Cage movies cause people to drown in swimming pools.

This flaw should be painfully obvious. This argument is silly. Things can be correlated without there being any actual correlation. That is the case here. Whenever the LSAT brings in a correlation, you need to know that we can not conclude causation based on only that evidence. This flaw will appear on every LR section, so make sure you know how to spot it.

Whole to Part (and vice versa)

The third flaw you will see on every LSAT test is the whole-to-part flaw. This flaw involves the test pointing out that a subset of a group has a quality, and therefore the whole group has that quality. They can also make a generalization about a group and then apply it to an individual group member. Let's do an example of each so that you can see how it looks.

US States typically get snowfall. Therefore, Hawaii, a US state, gets snowfall.

Ask yourself, is this whole to part, or part to whole? Are we over-generalizing from an individual, or are we applying a broad generalization to an individual group member?

This argument here is whole to part. We know that, on average, most US states get snowfall. However, we cannot conclude that they all get snowfall. There will be outliers such as Arizona and Hawaii that do not get snowfall, so applying the generalization that US states get snowfall to any US state is not logically valid. This argument is an example of whole to part.

Let's do another one.

San Francisco is foggy. San Francisco is in California. Therefore, California is all foggy.

So here, our premise is that San Francisco is foggy. With premises in LR, we do not want to argue with the truth of the premise. Whether or not San Francisco is foggy in real life is irrelevant to the objection we want to make on the LSAT. The second sentence is a premise again. San Francisco is in California. As a premise, we cannot object here. Even if it had said, "San Francisco is on the moon," we would not have grounds to object. We must wait for them to conclude something false based on this evidence.

The final sentence is where they go off the rails and make their nonsense conclusion. They say that all of California is foggy. Those who are familiar with California should be somewhat puzzled by this statement. California is not all foggy. Parts of it are, such as San Francisco, but California is a rather large state, so we can not make such a broad conclusion. This argument is an example of a part to whole flaw.

Spotting Flaws

So we've covered the three most common LSAT flaws, but the LSAT can make BS arguments in various ways. You do not need to memorize them. Instead, whenever the LSAT makes a nonsense argument, you should be able to object in plain English.

For the correct answer, you'll have to often translate your plain objection to a more "LSAT jargon" way of saying the answer. Let's do an example.

PT22 Section 3 Question 9

Television news coverage gives viewers a sense of direct involvement with current events but does not provide the depth of coverage needed for the significance of those events to be appreciated. Newspapers, on the other hand, provide depth of coverage but no sense of direct involvement. Unfortunately, a full understanding of current events requires both an appreciation of their significance and a sense of direct involvement with them. Therefore, since few people seek out news sources other than newspapers and television, few people ever fully understand current events.

Our job is to determine whether their conclusion has followed from the premises they gave up. If it has, it's a valid argument. However, we will usually have an objection. At this point, do you have an objection? Ask yourself this and think about this argument before you read my thoughts on this argument.

Alright, let's break down this argument sentence by sentence. The first sentence is, "Television news coverage gives viewers a sense of direct involvement with current events but does not provide the depth of coverage needed for the significance of those events to be appreciated." This sentence is a premise. They tell us that TV news gives the viewer a sense of involvement but does not give significance. Even though we cannot argue with a premise, we still want to react to what they are saying. So we know that when people consume news through television, they feel involved. Perhaps the visual of the new story allows people to feel like they are experiencing what is going on. They tell us that the depth of coverage is not good enough for appreciation. At this point, I think that a segment on TV can show what is happening but does not communicate the gravity of the situation. Perhaps a TV news segment on flooding displays how severe the flooding is, but the context is left out. We do not know whether this is a typical situation or whether it is a flood that only happens once every 1000 years.

They then tell us, "Newspapers, on the other hand, provide depth of coverage but no sense of direct involvement." So, newspapers are the opposite of television. We know that newspapers communicate depth, but they do not make readers feel like they are genuinely in the moment. This idea makes sense; each source of news has its deficiency. Perhaps, a solid news consumer could use both to understand the situation and have a direct sense of involvement.

They finish the argument by saying, "Therefore, since few people seek out news sources other than newspapers and television, few people ever fully understand current events." This conclusion makes no sense, given our premises. Even though it is true that few people seek out news sources other than newspapers and television, we could have all of those people consuming both of these sources. If this were true, the conclusion would make no sense. The conclusion is predicated upon the fact that people can only consume one news source, but the argument never established this premise. If we could add the premise that "Most people consume only one news source," the premises would prove the conclusion. However, we do not have that sentence, so we have a gaping hole.

Let's put this flaw in our own words. I might say, "assumes that a person can only consume one form of news." The LSAT will likely give us the answer differently, but it will mean the same thing.

Now that we've identified the flaw we can read the question.

The reasoning in the argument is flawed because the argument

This question is a flaw question, so they are asking us to identify what the argument has done wrong. Let's take a look at our answers.

A. Treats two things, neither one of which can plausibly be seen as excluding the other, as though they were mutually exclusive
B. Ignores the possibility that people read newspapers or watch television for reasons other than gaining a full understanding of current events
C. Makes crucial use of the term "depth of coverage" without defining it
D. Fails to consider the possible disadvantages of having a sense of direct involvement with tragic or violent events
E. Mistakenly reasons that just because something has the capacity to perform a given function it actually does so

Take a second and think about which of these answers describes the flaw we identified. Here, the flaw was "assumes a person can only consume one form of news." We'll review them individually to see if they describe that flaw.

A seems pretty good. Here, we treat the two things (watching TV and reading the news) as mutually exclusive. There is no reason to believe that these things are mutually exclusive; hence, this is the flaw we are looking for. This answer is another way of saying what we predicted: that a person can only consume one form of news. While a little jargony, this is what we anticipated.

B is wrong because we don't care why people are watching television. We care about treating TV and reading newspapers as mutually exclusive. The motivation for people to consume news is irrelevant.

C is wrong because we are not using the term "depth of coverage" abstractly. We can assume that depth of coverage here refers to context and implications. This is not some crazy abstract term that the reader cannot understand; hence, it is not a flaw.

D is wrong because we do not care about the drawbacks of consuming news. We care about whether or not people can have both depth of coverage and direct involvement. Tragedy has nothing to do with this.

E is wrong because it's talking nonsense. Here, we have to ask ourselves what we are even referring to. Here, we are not saying that "TV can cause happiness. Therefore every person that watches TV will be happy." That's an example of that flaw, and it is simply not what is happening in this question.

That should make sense. We do not need to memorize a list of flaws to approach the LR section properly, but we need a healthy BS detector. Object when the arguments don't make sense and explain why it doesn't make sense in English. If you can do that, you will demolish LR.

Other Flaws that Come Up

We do not need to memorize flaws on the LSAT, but some will come up often. Some of these come up mostly as wrong answers, so let's discuss them quickly.

Circular Reasoning

Circular reasoning is a simple flaw. In this flaw, the argument will use the same evidence as both a conclusion and a premise. It is SO apparent when the test does this, so I'll give you a quick example.

Sixteen years olds are allowed to drive because they are 16 years old.

This argument doesn't tell us anything. We know that 16-year-olds can drive because (in the states) that is the age that it is legal to drive. However, our nonsense argument here just said that 16-year-olds can drive because they are 16. This argument is nonsense and uses circular reasoning.

Like many of these less common flaws, circular reasoning is self-evident and rarely on the LSAT. This flaw will be a wrong answer choice more often than a correct one. If you didn't spot it in the argument, it is doubtful that the flaw in an argument is circular reasoning.

Ad Hominems

An ad hominem attacks a speaker rather than addressing their argument. This flaw is super common in real life. I'll quickly show an example.

We should reject Senator Bob's proposal to build a new park. Senator Bob is having an affair on his wife. We must therefore reject his call for a new park.

The flaw here should be super obvious. While it sucks that Senator Bob is having an affair on his wife, this is irrelevant to his suggestion that we build a new park. It will be this obvious on the actual LSAT. Similar to circular reasoning, this mostly appears as a wrong answer choice.

Sample Size

Like the other flaws in this section, sample size typically appears as a wrong answer. The good news for you is that this flaw has to be obvious for the LSAT to have it as the correct answer.

This flaw will make a broad conclusion based on limited evidence. It often shows up as a wrong answer, but here's what it would look like.

I asked all ten of my neighbors who they would vote for in the next national election. They all said they would vote for Candidate A over Candidate B. Therefore, Candidate A will win the national election.

Here, we can not conclude that Candidate A will win the election. The voting patterns of my neighbors will not decide the election. The sample we are using does not justify the conclusion. Like the other flaws in this chapter, a sample size flaw is super obvious when you run into it and appears much more often as an incorrect answer choice.

Use of a Key Term

Use of a key term is where the argument will use one word in two different ways. Typically, it's a word that has multiple definitions. In a premise, they'll use one definition, and in the conclusion, they'll use a different definition. These, like our other flaws here, are super obvious. I'll show a quick example.

Bob's favorite animal is a crane. Therefore, Bob is likely to want to operate a crane as his career.

Now, this argument is dumb. We know that cranes are a type of bird and that cranes are also a type of construction vehicle. The only thing these two objects have in common is that the word we use to refer to them is identical. This LSAT flaw is often a wrong answer but rarely shows up as the actual flaw the argument makes.

Final Thoughts on Flaws

Identifying flaws on the LSAT is something you need to get good at. The good news is that you can boil it down to one question.

Do the premises provided prove the conclusion the argument makes?

Often, the answer will be no. The answer to many LSAT questions is how the premises do not prove the conclusion. You don't have to memorize these flaws, but instead, be a critical reader. Familiarity with these flaws can be helpful, but for the most part, you just want to be able to say, in English, what the flaw is in an argument before you even read the answers.

Logical Reasoning Examples

Logical Reasoning Examples

Now that you're familiar with the common flaws you'll see on the LSAT, let's do a bunch of LR questions to see how you execute our approach.

On LR, read the argument first. You want to attack it throughout and determine where the argument has weaknesses or if the argument makes any blatant flaws. You do not want to agree with the argument. Sometimes you'll run into a valid argument, but you should be surprised if this happens.

After reading the question, you should then predict the answer mentally before you even read what they have written. If you know what you are looking for, you can quickly move through the wrong answers.

Question 1

In this segment, we'll be going through actual LR questions. Read the argument yourself first, and ask yourself the following questions.

1. Does this argument make sense?
2. Is there a flaw?
3. Could I bring in any evidence that would weaken it?
4. Could I bring in any evidence to strengthen it?

PT19 Section 2 Question 1

Director of Ace Manufacturing Company: Our management consultant proposes that we reassign staff so that all employees are doing both what they like to do and what they do well. This, she says, will "increase productivity by fully exploiting our available resources." But Ace Manufacturing has a long-standing commitment not to exploit its workers. Therefore, implementing her recommendations would cause us to violate our own policy.

Now, you should ensure you're not just reading the words on the page. You NEED to react to what is said. Did you react? If you didn't, go back and reread it.

Alright, hopefully, you've reacted. We'll go through it together to see how your reactions align with mine.

We know that the speaker is the Director of Ace Manufacturing Company. We don't have much of a reaction to this since we know nothing about this position or company, but it is important to note who is making this claim.

They start the argument by saying, "Our management consultant proposes that we reassign staff so that all employees are doing both what they like to do and what they do well." At this point, we want to recognize that this is simply a fact. The management consultant is making a suggestion. We might think the suggestion is dumb, but we cannot argue with the truth of this claim. I also believe that this suggestion tends to make sense. If employees are doing things they enjoy and are good at, I expect productivity to be good.

They continue by saying, "This, she says, will "increase productivity by fully exploiting our available resources." Once again, we have a premise. However, we want to note that the argument says the management consultant is making a claim. Often, on the LSAT, when the argument says someone is making a claim, it's setting up an attack on that claim. Perhaps our speaker is about to say why the management consultant is wrong. At this point, I am inclined to agree with the management consultant. Assigning employees to tasks they are good at and enjoy seems to be the optimal way to run a company.

The argument continues with, "But Ace Manufacturing has a long-standing commitment not to exploit its workers." This sentence is a premise once again. As a premise, we have to accept it, but we can still react. It makes sense that Ace Manufacturing should not exploit its workers, but this seems irrelevant to the management consultant's statement. Our consultant just said that we should exploit available resources. When she says this, I picture an efficient use of resources where time/energy is not wasted. Our speaker misinterprets this as saying we should "exploit workers." I picture sweatshops or incredibly long hours when I think of exploiting workers. These situations are not what our management consultant is talking about, so our speaker's reaction to their claim is odd.

Our speaker concludes, "Therefore, implementing her recommendations would cause us to violate our own policy." At this point, we want to react. Our speaker has made a nonsense argument. We have used the word "exploit" in two entirely different ways. This is a flaw in the argument.

Now that we've digested the argument, we want to examine the question. We are ready to answer no matter what the LSAT throws at us because we fully comprehend what is going on.

The director's argument for rejecting the management consultant's proposal is most vulnerable to criticism on which one of the following grounds?

This question is a flaw question. The LSAT is asking us what the argument did. At this point, we want to ask ourselves if we spotted the flaw, and we want to predict the answer. Generally, we should have spotted the flaw in the argument on flaw questions.

My prediction for this answer would be that "the argument used the word "exploit" in two entirely different ways." They'll often phrase the answers in a more jargony way, but it will hit that idea.

If we cannot see the flaw in the argument, we want to ask ourselves the following two questions as we go through the answers.

1. Did the argument do this?
2. Is that even a flaw?

Sometimes the argument will do something like "fails to consider that exploitation is not the most egregious thing a company can do." Technically, our argument did that. However, it is not a flaw because we do not care what is egregious and what is not. We care about whether or not our company is violating its own policies.

Alright, now that we know what we are looking for, let's look at these answers.

A. Failing to distinguish two distinct senses of a key term

B. Attempting to defend an action on the ground that it is frequently carried out
C. Defining a term by pointing to an atypical example of something to which the term applies
D. Drawing a conclusion that simply restates one of the premises of the argument
E. Calling something by a less offensive term than the term that is usually used to name one thing

Which of these answers matches the flaw we spotted? One does, and four do not. You should be able to figure it out at this point.

A matches our prediction. The flaw we spotted is that the argument uses the word "exploit" in two different ways. A is describing that flaw.

B is wrong because we are not defending an action. This could be a flaw, but our argument did not do this, so it fails Question 1 of our flaw questions.

C is wrong because we are not defining a term by pointing to an atypical example. We are not even defining a term, so this fails Question 1 of our flaw questions.

D is wrong because this is not circular reasoning. We covered this in Chapter 2, but circular reasoning does not look like this.

E is wrong because we are not calling anything by a less offensive term. If anything, we are calling it by a more offensive term and claiming that Ace Manufacturing is exploiting its workers by using them efficiently, so E also fails Question 1.

Question 2

As a reminder, here are the questions we want to be thinking through. You do not have to answer every single one of these literally, but have these questions in the back of your mind as you read. If you just read critically, you can disregard these, but I'll include them so that as you are practicing, you can refer back to them.

1. Does this argument make sense?
2. Is there a flaw?
3. Could I bring in any evidence that would weaken it?
4. Could I bring in any evidence to strengthen it?

PT19 Section 3 Question 9

Measurements of the motion of the planet Uranus seem to show Uranus being tugged by a force pulling it away from the Sun and the inner planets. Neptune and Pluto, the two known planets whose orbits are farther from the Sun than is the orbit of Uranus, do not have enough mass to exert the force that the measurements indicate. Therefore, in addition to known planets, there must be at least one planet in our solar system that we have yet to discover.

Ensure you've read this actively and reacted to what the argument says. Let's go through it together so you can compare your thought process to mine.

They start by saying, "Measurements of the motion of the planet Uranus seem to show Uranus being tugged by a force pulling it away from the Sun and the inner planets." Here we are given a fact. We know that something is pulling Uranus away from the Sun. That seems odd. I thought planets had relatively fixed orbits, so this is weird. Perhaps it has been knocked off track by a giant asteroid, or maybe we miscalculated the orbit of Uranus in the first place.

They continue by saying, "Neptune and Pluto, the two known planets whose orbits are farther from the Sun than is the orbit of Uranus, do not have enough mass to exert the force that the measurements indicate." Once again, this is simply a fact. They are just telling us that Neptune and Pluto are not the explanation for what is happening here. That doesn't mean that the change in orbit is not happening; it just means that Neptune and Pluto are not the cause.

They conclude, "Therefore, in addition to known planets, there must be at least one planet in our solar system that we have yet to discover." This conclusion makes no sense. Even in my initial reaction, I thought of other ways Uranus could have altered its trajectory other than a gravitational pull. Maybe it was hit by an asteroid. Perhaps aliens are using a tractor beam on it. Whether it's plausible or silly, it doesn't matter. The vital thing to note here is that they have not proven their argument, so we want to attack on those grounds.

Now let's read the question.

Which one of the following, if true, most seriously weakens the argument?

This is a weaken question. We are trying to hurt the argument by bringing in outside info. With a weakener, we can bring in all sorts of external information. I have several predictions.
1. An asteroid affected the trajectory of Uranus
2. Aliens are using their tractor beam on Uranus
3. There are objects other than planets that can exert a gravitational pull.

Now the correct answer could match one of my predictions or be something entirely new. It just needs to weaken their conclusion that there is a planet we don't know about that is causing Uranus to be moving.

Let's take a look at the answers.

  A. Pluto was not discovered until 1930.
  B. There is a belt of comets beyond the orbit of Pluto with powerful gravitational pull.
  C. Neither Neptune nor Pluto is as massive as Uranus.
  D. The force the Sun exerts on Uranus is weaker than the force it exerts on inner planets.
  E. Uranus' orbit is closer to Neptune's orbit than it is to Pluto's.

Take a moment to think about which of these ideas weakens our argument. We are trying to weaken the idea that there is some mystery planet influencing Uranus' trajectory.

A is irrelevant. We do not care when Pluto was discovered. We care about what is affecting Uranus.

B is pretty good. If there were a belt of comets beyond Pluto that exerted a gravitational pull, that would explain why Uranus is moving. It would also explain that it's not a planet affecting Uranus but instead a comet belt.

C is wrong because we've already established that these planets are not affecting Uranus in our premises.

D is also irrelevant because we don't care why the Sun isn't as strong on Uranus as it is on Earth. We care about why Uranus is being pulled in the other direction, and this answer does not help us.

E is wrong because we do not care how close Uranus is to Neptune or Pluto. Their location in the solar system is irrelevant here.

Question 3

The cumbersome spears that were the principal weapons used by certain tribes in the early Bronze Age precluded widespread casualties during intertribal conflicts. But the comparatively high number of warrior tombs found in recent excavations of the same tribes' late Bronze Age settlements indicate that in the late Bronze Age wars between these tribes were frequent, and the casualty rate was high. Hence some archaeologists claim that by the late Bronze Age, these tribes had developed new methods of warfare designed to inflict many casualties.

Take a moment to have your reaction.

The argument starts by saying, "The cumbersome spears that were the principal weapons used by certain tribes in the early Bronze Age precluded widespread casualties during intertribal conflicts." This sentence is a premise, and they are simply telling us that the spears used in the early Bronze Age were not effective. Because these spears were cumbersome, it was hard for the tribes to kill each other, so there was not as much death. Make sure you are breaking down the ideas and understanding the idea here. Don't get lost in words like precluded. Figure it out and if you need to reread, take the time to do so. You are smart enough to figure this out, but you must understand every sentence you read.

The argument continues, "But the comparatively high number of warrior tombs found in recent excavations of the same tribes' late Bronze Age settlements indicate that in the late Bronze Age wars between these tribes were frequent, and the casualty rate was high." Now we know that as the Bronze Age progressed, more people died. I am guessing that the weapons got better. We understand that the spears were keeping the casualty rate low. Still, perhaps better technology has helped these tribes get better at killing each other. Perhaps it's better spears, or maybe a new weapon like a sword.

The argument concludes, "Hence some archaeologists claim that by the late Bronze Age, these tribes had developed new methods of warfare designed to inflict many casualties." This conclusion makes sense, but we have not proven this argument. There could be higher casualties even with the old spears. Perhaps the tribes just got mad at each other and, despite their poor weapons, still killed each other a bunch. It's not likely, but it's possible, so they have not proven their conclusion.

Let's take a look at the question.

Which one of the following, if true, most supports the archaeologists' claim?

This is a strengthen question and is the opposite of a weakener. Like a weakener, we get to bring in outside info. This time, we are trying to make the argument better, though. I have a few predictions.
1. We found swords in the warrior tombs.
2. Geological archives show a transition from stone to steel in weapons at this time.
3. Carbon dating of the cumbersome spears shows that warriors no longer used them during this time of higher casualty warfare.

The answer doesn't have to match my predictions, but it will be along those lines. Let's take a look at our answers.

A. A royal tomb dating to the early Bronze Age contained pottery depicting battle scenes in which warriors use spears.
B. There is evidence that many buildings dating to the late Bronze Age were built by prisoners of war taken in battles between enemy tribes.

C. Scenes of violent warfare, painted in bright hues, frequently appear on pottery that has been found in some early Bronze Age tombs of warriors.

D. Some tombs of warriors dating to the late Bronze Age contain armor and weapons that anthropologists believe were trophies taken from enemies in battle.

E. The marks on the bones of many of the late Bronze Age warriors whose tombs were excavated are consistent with the kind of wounds inflicted by arrowheads also found in many late Bronze Age settlements.

Take a moment to think through these answers and which one best strengthens the idea that there was a new kind of warfare.

A is wrong because what is depicted on pottery does not matter. We are also trying to figure out what is happening in the late Bronze Age, and here they are talking about the early Bronze Age. Further, they are talking about spears, and we want a new form of weaponry. A is wrong for three different reasons.

B is wrong because we do not care who is building things.

C is wrong because these scenes of violent warfare cover the early Bronze Age. Also, they do not introduce a new form of warfare which is what we are looking for.

D is wrong because we do not care that people took trophies from battle. We care about whether they are using new weaponry.

E is the correct answer here because it introduces a new method of warfare explaining the increased casualties. That method is arrows, which does not directly match our prediction. Hopefully, you can see how it parallels the sword prediction and functionally plays the same role as a strengthener.

Question 4

Faced with a financial crisis, Upland University's board of trustees reduced the budget for the university's computer center from last year's $4 million to $1.5 million for the coming year. However the center cannot operate on less than $2.5 million. Since the board cannot divert funds from other programs to the computer center, there is no way that the center can be kept operating for the coming year.

As usual, read this argument and ask yourself how you could attack it.

The argument starts with "Faced with a financial crisis, Upland University's board of trustees reduced the budget for the university's computer center from last year's $4 million to $1.5 million for the coming year." You should quickly recognize that this is simply a fact. All we know is that the university reduced the budget for the university's computer center. Make sure you are having a broader reaction to this fact. Why are they cutting the budget? Is this part of a more significant university budget cut? Is the economy taking a downturn?

The argument continues by saying, "However the center cannot operate on less than $2.5 million." We now know that this budget cut will lead to some real problems. We know our budget is now only $1.5 million, which is less than the center needs to operate. Perhaps the center is going to stop running. However, they could also cut staff, change operations, or modify their practices to work within this new budget.

The argument concludes, "Since the board cannot divert funds from other programs to the computer center, there is no way that the center can be kept operating for the coming year." This conclusion, as per usual, has not been proven by our argument. Other ways besides diverting funds would allow the computer center to continue operating. Perhaps wealthy alums of the university will come into the picture and fund the computer center. The center could keep operating if funding came from other sources.

We now know how to attack this argument, so we can read the question.

The conclusion of the argument is properly drawn if which one of the following is assumed?

This is a sufficient assumption question, which is kind of like an overkill strengthener. We need to fix this argument and make it logically proven. Often, this type of question involves fixing the flaw that we spotted. As a quick refresher, the flaw we spotted is that there are other ways that the computer center could be funded besides diverting funds.

My predicted answer to fix this argument would be, "*There are no ways besides diverting funds that the computer center could be funded.*" If we were to insert that premise, our argument would make sense. Let's look at our answers and see if they help us.

A. The computer center did not use all of the $4 million that was budgeted to it last year.
B. The budgets of other programs at the university were also reduced.
C. The computer center has no source of funds other than those budgeted to it for the coming year by the university's board of trustees.
D. No funds from any program at the university can be diverted to other programs.
E. The board of trustees at the university value other programs at the university more highly than they do the computer center.

One of these matches what we predicted, and four do not. Take a second to identify the correct answer.

A is wrong because we do not care that the computer center did not use all $4 million. The budget cut to $1.5 million would still be a real problem for the computer center since it requires $2.5 million to operate. This answer does not prove our conclusion when added to our original argument.

B is wrong because we do not care if the fine arts department or athletics had their budgets cut. This is irrelevant.

C is correct because it says that the only funding comes from the board of trustees. We know the board of trustees is not providing enough funding for the computer center to operate. This answer now tells us that the board of trustees is the only source of financing, and now we know that our conclusion is proven. It's worth noting that this is what we predicted.

D is wrong because this does not prove our conclusion at all. We have already established that the computer center will not be saved by diverting funds, so explaining why that diversion cannot happen does not matter.

E is wrong because we do not care what the board values. Perhaps they value the computer center, but overall budget cuts require cuts to all departments. This answer does not prove our argument.

Question 5

Braille is a method of producing text by means of raised dots that can be read by touch. A recent development in technology will allow flat computer screens to be made of a material that can be heated in patterns that replicate the patterns used in braille. Since the thermal device will utilize the same symbol system as braille, it follows that anyone who is accustomed to reading braille can easily adapt to the use of this electronic system.

Did this argument make sense to you?

It didn't to me, so if you found yourself agreeing with what the argument was saying, stop. Go back, and figure out what you missed. If you don't strongly oppose this argument, you read it too passively.

The argument starts by saying, "Braille is a method of producing text by means of raised dots that can be read by touch." Here, the argument defines braille. Nothing really to react to here other than to take note of what braille is.

The argument continues, "A recent development in technology will allow flat computer screens to be made of a material that can be heated in patterns that replicate the patterns used in braille." This sentence is once again just a fact, but we can have more of a reaction to this. I am skeptical that reading heated patterns will be as easy as reading raised bumps. Just because we can heat screens in such a way does not mean that people will be able to read heated patterns like they can read braille bumps.

The argument concludes, "Since the thermal device will utilize the same symbol system as braille, it follows that anyone who is accustomed to reading braille can easily adapt to the use of this electronic system." This is dumb. Can people distinguish heated patterns like they can distinguish raised bumps?

We have our primary objection, so we can move into the question.

Which one of the following is an assumption on which the conclusion depends?

This is a necessary assumption question. The correct answer will be something the argument has to agree with. However, our correct answer will not necessarily make our argument better. The correct answer is just something that this argument must depend on.

The good news is that our flaw fits perfectly as a necessary assumption. A good prediction here would be, "People that can read braille using bumps can also read thermal patterns as braille."

Let's read our answers.

    A. Braille is the only system that can be readily adapted for use with the new thermal screen.
    B. Only people who currently use braille as their sole medium for reading text will have the capacity to adapt to the use of the thermal screen.
    C. People with the tactile ability to discriminate symbols in braille have an ability to discriminate similar patterns on a flat heated surface.
    D. Some symbol systems encode a piece of text by using dots that replicate the shape of letters of the alphabet.
    E. Eventually, it will be possible to train people to read braille by first training them in the use of the thermal screen.

One of these matches our prediction, so make sure you can spot it.

A is wrong because the argument does not have to agree with this. Perhaps we can translate other symbols to thermal screens. They never say that we can only use this technology for braille.

B is wrong because it does not have to be true that the only people who use this new system are those who only read in braille. Perhaps sighted people that also know braille can use this new thermal system. Our speaker does not have to agree with this.

C is exactly what we predicted. Our objection was, "Can people that read braille even use this thermal system?" C answers this by saying yes, they can.

D is wrong because we do not care about other symbol systems. These symbol systems do not need to exist for our argument to make sense, so our speaker does not have to agree with this.

E is wrong because we do not have to agree that this will be a training tool. Our speaker does not have to agree with it, which means it cannot be our answer to a necessary assumption question.

Question 6

All bridges built from 1950 to 1960 are in serious need of rehabilitation. Some bridges constructed in this period, however, were built according to faulty engineering design. That is the bad news. The good news is that at least some of the bridges in serious need of rehabilitation are not suspension bridges, since no suspension bridges are among the bridges that were built according to faulty engineering design.

What was your reaction to this argument? You should have noticed that they do not make a conclusion. Instead, this is a set of facts.

Let's break it down. "All bridges built from 1950 to 1960 are in serious need of rehabilitation." This is simply a fact. Every single bridge from this time period needs rehabilitation. Note this and continue.

"Some bridges constructed in this period, however, were built according to faulty engineering design." We also know that some of these bridges had faulty engineering designs. "Some" is abstract and could refer to either very few or many of these bridges. Either way, we know there is at least some subset of these bridges that were built using poor engineering designs.

"The good news is that at least some of the bridges in serious need of rehabilitation are not suspension bridges, since no suspension bridges are among the bridges that were built according to faulty engineering design." We now know that there are at least two types of bridges: suspension and other. According to our second sentence, all faulty engineering bridges are other bridges.

With sets of facts like this, we need to understand each sentence. The questions tend to be a bit more open-ended after such an argument.

However, we still need to have understood everything that the argument says. I don't have a significant objection here, but I have digested what they've said, so we can read the question at this point.

If the statements above are true, then, on the basis of those statements, which one of the following must also be true?

This is a must-be true question, and it's precisely what it looks like. Given what the argument has told us, we must find the answer that must follow. We can't predict these because they can go in all sorts of directions, but we can quickly think about what would have to be true.

For example, a prediction could be, *"At least some of the bridges in need of repair are not suspension bridges."* This is not the only possible answer; they could go in a completely different direction and talk about faulty engineering standards, for example. With these, we have to go answer by answer and ask ourselves, "Does that have to be true?"

A. Some suspension bridges are not in serious need of rehabilitation.
B. Some suspension bridges are in serious need of rehabilitation.
C. Some bridges that were built according to faulty engineering design are in serious need of rehabilitation.
D. Some bridges built from 1950 to 1960 are not in serious need of rehabilitation.
E. Some bridges that were built according to faulty engineering designs are not bridges other than suspension bridges.

Remember that the answer we pick here has to be 100% provable. A possibility is not good enough. We need an answer that is certain.

A is wrong because we never talk about bridges that do not need rehabilitation.

B is wrong because we never say that suspension bridges were built in the 1950s or 1960s. Since the bridges constructed in that time period are the only ones we know of that need rehabilitation, we cannot prove B.

C is correct because we know that some bridges built from 1950 to 1960 had faulty engineering designs. We also understand that every bridge built in that period needs repairs. Therefore, we know that some of the bridges built with faulty engineering designs must need rehabilitation.

D is wrong because we know that every bridge from that period needs rehabilitation.

E is wrong because it's saying that some of the bridges built under faulty engineering designs are suspension bridges. We say the exact opposite in our argument, so this can never be true.

Question 7

In a recession, a decrease in consumer spending causes many businesses to lay off workers or even to close. Workers who lose their jobs in a recession usually cannot find new jobs. The result is an increase in the number of people who are jobless. Recovery from a recession is defined by an increase in consumer spending and an expansion of business activity that creates a need for additional workers. But businesspeople generally have little confidence in the economy after a recession and therefore delay hiring additional workers as long as possible.

What was your reaction to this argument? Once again, this is more of a set of facts than an argument. However, we can see where this argument is going more clearly than we could with the last argument. With a set of statements like this, we can see how the statements tie together to make a logical conclusion.

The argument starts, "In a recession, a decrease in consumer spending causes many businesses to lay off workers or even to close." At this point, you should know that this is a fact, and we cannot argue with it. This fact does make sense. We know that, in recessions, people spend less money, which can hurt businesses.

"The result is an increase in the number of people who are jobless." This also makes sense. When there is less spending, it's harder for businesses to employ people.

"Recovery from a recession is defined by an increase in consumer spending and an expansion of business activity that creates a need for additional workers." Now they are defining what recovery is. We can see that to have a recovery, consumers need to be spending more money, and businesses need to expand to create a need for additional workers. Note here that demand for additional workers does not equal more jobs. It is simply demand. Businesses could delay the actual hiring back of new workers.

"But businesspeople generally have little confidence in the economy after a recession and therefore delay hiring additional workers as long as possible." They now tell us that businesspeople are apprehensive to hire back workers after the recession. At this point, we can tie our facts together to say, in our words, how we would finish the argument.

I would say, *"Therefore, in recoveries, jobs do not come back immediately."* As always, with our predictions, this can be worded separately from what they will say, but the general idea should be similar. Now, let's see what they are even asking us.

The statements above, if true, provide most support for which one of the following conclusions?

This is a most strongly supported question. Here, the LSAT asks us what would make sense to add to the end of the argument. We have already identified how to tie the facts together to create a logical conclusion, so we have our prediction. This question has a lower standard than a must-be true because we don't have to 100% prove our answer, but it needs to tie our premises together. The wrong answers here will bring in new stuff that we didn't discuss.

A. Recessions are usually caused by a decrease in businesspeople's confidence in the economy.
B. Governmental intervention is required in order for an economy to recover from a recession.
C. Employees of businesses that close during a recession make up the majority of the workers who lose their jobs during that recession.
D. Sometimes recovery from a recession does not promptly result in a decrease in the number of people who are jobless.

E. Workers who lose their jobs during a recession are likely to get equally good jobs when the economy recovers.

Which of these ties the premises together? Which of these brings in new info that we don't care about?

A is wrong because we never talk about what causes recessions.

B is wrong because we never talk about governmental intervention.

C is wrong because we do not care about the proportion of people that lose their jobs due to layoffs versus businesses closing.

D is correct because this ties our premises together. We talk about how businesses delay hiring workers even though things start to recover. D says this can sometimes happen, which is supported by our argument.

E is wrong because we never talk about the quality of jobs.

Question 8

More women than men suffer from Alzheimer's disease—a disease that is most commonly contracted by elderly persons. This discrepancy has often been attributed to women's longer life span, but this theory may be wrong. A recent study has shown that prescribing estrogen to women after menopause, when estrogen production in the body decreases, may prevent them from developing the disease. Men's supply of testosterone may help safeguard them against Alzheimer's disease because much of it is converted by the body to estrogen, and testosterone levels stay relatively stable into old age.

As usual, take a minute to react.

"More women than men suffer from Alzheimer's disease—a disease that is most commonly contracted by elderly persons." You already know what this is. It's a premise. Here, we know that more women than men get Alzheimer's disease.

"This discrepancy has often been attributed to women's longer life span, but this theory may be wrong." They now tell us another fact, which is a past explanation for why women more often get Alzheimer's than men. They also add a conclusion by saying that this theory might be wrong. I don't know much about Alzheimer's and what causes it, so I don't have a strong reaction to whether or not the explanation of women living longer is a good or bad explanation for why women get it more. Our author seems to think that there might be an alternative explanation. I don't know if they are right or wrong, so now we have to evaluate the evidence they provide.

"A recent study has shown that prescribing estrogen to women after menopause, when estrogen production in the body decreases, may prevent them from developing the disease." They are bringing in new info here and telling us that we have a new study telling us that by giving women extra estrogen, we can lower the odds of them developing Alzheimer's. This evidence is solid supporting evidence, but we can still have objections. Was the study run properly? Did they use a representative set of women? Are there any confounding variables that could mess with the results?

"Men's supply of testosterone may help safeguard them against Alzheimer's disease because much of it is converted by the body to estrogen, and testosterone levels stay relatively stable into old age." This sentence is more evidence for their conclusion because it gives us a reason why men don't need supplemental estrogen to prevent Alzheimer's. Men keep producing estrogen into their old age, so they do not need supplements.

My main objection here would be to the quality of the study. It's not a flaw because we do not know that the researchers did the study poorly, but if this were a weaken question, calling the study into question would be an excellent attack point. Let's read the question to see what they want us to do.

Which one of the following most accurately expresses the main conclusion of the argument?

Ok, so they are simply asking us to identify what the conclusion is. By reading the argument, we should know this immediately.

The whole point of this argument was to say, *"Women do not get Alzheimer's more than men because they live longer."*

If you have trouble identifying the conclusion, you must ask yourself why the argument exists. What is it trying to say? We have our prediction at this point, so we can find the correct answer here and be done.

A. A decrease in estrogen, rather than longer life span, may explain the higher occurrence of Alzheimer's disease in women relative to men.
B. As one gets older, one's chances of developing Alzheimer's disease increase.
C. Women who go through menopause earlier in life than do most other women have an increased risk of contracting Alzheimer's disease.
D. The conversion of testosterone into estrogen may help safeguard men from Alzheimer's disease.
E. Testosterone is necessary for preventing Alzheimer's disease in older men.

A is right because this is precisely what our argument was trying to prove. The whole point of the argument is to get rid of an older explanation for why women get Alzheimer's and replace it with a new one.

B is wrong because this is a premise.

C is wrong because this is not the conclusion. They don't even really say this, although we could infer it.

D is wrong because this is a premise.

E is wrong because we don't even know that this is true. Testosterone can help, but it may not be necessary. Either way, it's not the conclusion we are looking for.

Question 9

Many people are alarmed about the population explosion. They fail to appreciate that the present rise in population has in fact been followed by equally potent economic growth. Because of this connection between an increase in population and an increase in economic activity, population control measures should not be taken.

Make sure as you read this argument, you thought about what possible ways you could attack it. If you are not doing this, LR will be hard. If you are, LR is going to be easy.

The argument starts, "Many people are alarmed about the population explosion." This sentence is a premise, and we need to accept that it is true. The one reaction I do have is their use of "many." "Many" is an ambiguous term and does not tell us much. Many people could refer to three people or all people. As a quantifier, it does not tell us much.

"They fail to appreciate that the present rise in population has in fact been followed by equally potent economic growth." This sentence is an attack on the people that are concerned. Our speaker is saying that these silly people worried about population growth are failing to consider that past population growth has led to economic growth. Now, I see a pretty glaring issue with this argument. Just because two things are correlated does not mean one caused the other. Even if population growth caused economic growth in the past, this relationship could stop being true in the future. It might, but we don't know whether it will or not.

"Because of this connection between an increase in population and an increase in economic activity, population control measures should not be taken." Our speaker concludes by saying that we should not take population control measures. But they have not made a convincing argument with the evidence they provided. Their evidence is that past population growth has been correlated with economic growth. This conclusion is silly because two things being correlated does not mean they are causally related. It's possible that the population explosion and economic growth in the past had no causal relationship.

It comes back to the central idea that correlation doesn't equal causation. Our argument takes this for granted, and they are not allowed to do that. Your attack on this argument needs to be that this argument assumes from a correlation that there is causation. Let's read the question.

The questionable pattern of reasoning in the argument above is most similar to that in which one of the following?

This is a parallel flaw question. The question will give us five arguments, one of which will make the same flaw as our original argument. Since we've spotted the flaw in our argument, it should also be pretty easy to spot in the answers. To remind ourselves, we are looking for an argument that bases a course of action solely on a correlation.

A. Subscribers to newsmagazines are concerned that increased postage costs will be passed on to them in the form of higher subscription rates. But that is a price they have to pay for having the magazines delivered. No group of users of the postal system should be subsidized at the expense of others.

B. Most of the salespeople are concerned with complaints about the sales manager's aggressive behavior. They need to consider that sales are currently increasing. Due to this success, no action should be taken to address the manager's behavior.

C. Parents are concerned about their children spending too much time watching television. Those parents should consider television time a time they could spend with their children. Let the children watch television, but watch it with them.

D. Nutritionists warn people not to eat unhealthy foods. Those foods have been in people's diets for years. Before cutting all those foods out of diets it would be wise to remember that people enjoy culinary variety.

E. Some consumers become concerned when the price of a product increases for several years in a row, thinking that the price will continue to increase. But these consumers are mistaken since a long-term trend of price increases indicates that the price will probably decline in the future.

Remember, we are looking for them to say that because we have a correlation between two things, we should not do anything about something concerning.

A is wrong because this argument does not have a correlation. They are trying to justify the stamp increase, but the original argument had no such justification. We need a faulty correlation in our answer.

B is correct because they make a correlation between the sales manager's behavior and increasing sales. Here, the sales manager's behavior parallels the population explosion in the original argument. The increasing sales in this argument are parallel to the economic growth in the original argument. Similar to the original argument, this new argument states that because we have this beneficial thing (the increasing sales), we should not address a problem (the aggressive behavior of the sales manager). Here, they make the same flaw, basing a course of action on a faulty correlation.

C is wrong because they do not make any correlation.

D is wrong because they do not make any correlation.

E is wrong because they do not make any correlation. Based on past evidence, they are predicting what prices will do in the future. Still, they are not making an argument that we should ignore X because it is correlated with Y.

Question 10

Last year a large firm set a goal of decreasing its workforce by 25 percent. Three divisions, totaling 25 percent of its workforce at that time, were to be eliminated and no new people hired. These divisions have since been eliminated and no new people have joined the firm, but its workforce has decreased by only 15 percent.

Read this argument, identify the conclusion and figure out how you would attack it.

You should have noticed that there is no conclusion in this argument. Instead, we have three facts that seem in conflict with each other. Let's break it down.

"Last year a large firm set a goal of decreasing its workforce by 25 percent." This is a premise. We know that this firm wants to decrease its workforce. We should react to why they are bringing this up. Perhaps the economy is going through a recession. Maybe the bottom 25 percent of the workers are inefficient. Either way, you must understand that this firm plans to cut 25 percent of its workforce.

"Three divisions, totaling 25 percent of its workforce at that time, were to be eliminated and no new people hired." Now they tell us how the firm plans to reach its goal. It is going to cut three of its divisions. These three divisions equal 25 percent of the workforce. If the firm does indeed cut all these jobs, it should be able to reach its goal.

"These divisions have since been eliminated and no new people have joined the firm, but its workforce has decreased by only 15 percent." This is odd. If the firm did indeed cut these three divisions, yet the firm has not reached its goal, something has happened. We know the firm did not hire anyone else on, so in what ways could the firm have not reached its goal?

Perhaps the firm reassigned some employees from the cut divisions to other divisions. Even though the firm eliminated the three divisions, it could retain some employees, preventing the firm from reaching its employment cuts.

I'm expecting this to be a paradox question since we've spotted a paradox in the argument. Let's double-check by reading the question.

Which one of the following, if true, contributes most to an explanation of the difference in the planned versus the actual reduction in the workforce?

This is a paradox question. Paradox questions ask you to resolve a set of seemingly contradictory facts. You need to figure out, "why has the firm not decreased its overall employment by 25 percent despite cutting three divisions that makeup 25 percent of the firm's employment?"

Here, I predict that the firm transferred employees from the cut divisions to other divisions. This transfer would allow the firm to cut the three divisions entirely without cutting the whole workforce. Let's check out the answers.

A. The three divisions that were eliminated were well run and had the potential to earn profits.
B. Normal attrition in the retained divisions continued to reduce staff because no new people were added to the firm.
C. Some of the employees in the eliminated divisions were eligible for early retirement and chose that option.
D. As the divisions were being eliminated some of their employees were assigned to other divisions.
E. Employees in the retained divisions were forced to work faster to offset the loss of the eliminated divisions.

We are trying to explain our paradox. Our paradox is that we have cut three divisions which should have reduced the workforce by 25 percent. We know the firm only reduced the workforce by 15 percent, and we did not hire any new workers. We need to find an answer that explains why the firm did not reduce its workforce by 25 percent despite cutting three divisions.

A is wrong because we do not care about how useful and efficient the cut divisions were.

B is wrong because this would make our paradox more confusing. If the firm cut the three divisions and had normal attrition from our other divisions, we expect over 25 percent of the workforce to be gone, not less than 25 percent.

C is wrong because we do not care what happened to the people that left the company.

D is correct because it explains how even though the firm cut three divisions, it failed to cut all those jobs.

E is wrong because we do not care what effects this business move had on the other employees.

Closing Thoughts

Now that you've seen 10 LR questions fully explained, you should feel more confident about your ability to conquer this test section. These questions are little problems, and they are solvable.

These questions aren't meant to be tricks. People rush through them and make them harder than they are. You will do well on this test if you commit to understanding these arguments.

It's not about picking the best answer. It's about solving the argument and selecting the correct answer. As you go through LR, you are going to make mistakes. To get good at this test, you must accept that the LSAT is always right. This humility will allow you to see how the test works. That approach is how you get to never missing LR questions.

Reading Comprehension

Introduction to Reading Comprehension

In this section, we are going to go through reading comprehension. There are not a lot of tricks on reading comprehension. Instead, you need to do what the title of the section suggests. You need to read for comprehension.

Lawyers understand every word on the page. You need to take the same approach on these RC passages. Whenever you read an RC passage, you must understand every idea the LSAT throws at you. Read a sentence. Make sure you've understood it. Then move on. You are not allowed not to understand. Trying to do RC without understanding is planning to fail.

I don't focus on "indicator words" or "tone." If you understand what is going on, none of these things matter. I also don't focus on key ideas. There are no key ideas on LSAT RC. These passages are 15-20 sentences. Every idea is a key idea. You have to understand it all, so highlighting one idea as more important than others not only doesn't help you, it doesn't make sense.

In short, we will approach reading comprehension by simply trying to understand everything the LSAT says in the passages. When we do that, the questions become easy.

Reading Comprehension Basics

We will go through a passage and all its questions shortly. However, before doing that, I wanted to run through some reading comprehension concepts quickly.

Reading Comprehension Requires Comprehension

Reading comprehension involves dense passages. As I mentioned earlier, there is no way to approach RC other than to read for understanding. You do not need to focus on certain LSAT things, such as perspective or keywords. Instead, you must concentrate on each sentence and word and progress through the passage. Refuse not to understand.

You want to be a lawyer. When lawyers get a document dropped on their desks, they figure out what it means. There is no skimming for "key ideas" or getting the gist. Lawyers figure out what they are reading, and you need to too. Anything short of complete comprehension on the LSAT will result in missing questions.

Get Interested

These reading comprehension passages will talk about all sorts of things. Common topics include law, science, various arts, and social sciences. An easy way to do well on the LSAT is to learn about the topic.

If the passage is on French sculptures from the 17th century, try to learn. If you approach these passages with an open mind looking to learn, you don't even have to try to pay attention. Comprehension comes naturally as you try to learn about the topic.

You also should have reactions to what is said. Unlike in LR, we do not care whether the passage makes sense, but that doesn't mean we shouldn't be reacting. If you are reacting, it means you understand what you are reading. When the passage claims which sculptures are better, you should react. Perhaps you prefer marble, so their argument about how clay has a better aesthetic is silly. Your reaction is irrelevant, but the point is that you need to have one. If you are not reacting, you are being too passive on RC.

How to Answer the Questions

On RC, nearly all of the questions are "must be trues". This means that they need to be directly supportable by the passage. They will refer back to the passage and ask you something about it. These questions (with a few exceptions) require direct support from the passage. To pick an answer, you need to be able to point to the part of the passage that talks about what you are selecting. If you can't find an excerpt that supports your answer, why are you picking it? The LSAT does not want you to take any extra steps. It just wants you to parrot back at it what you've read.

The exceptions to this are strengtheners and weakeners. Sometimes, in RC, they ask you which of the following would weaken someone's argument. In these circumstances, you do not need support in the passage to pick your answer. You need to weaken the argument in these questions, as we discussed in the LR section.

I will illustrate this principle of supporting the answer as we go through a passage later in this section.

Spend Your Time on the Passage

A common mistake RC beginners make is rushing through the passage to get to the questions. While the motivations for this are understandable, it puts the test taker in a bad position. Test takers that speed through the passage do so at the expense of understanding what is happening. This approach makes it hard to answer the questions.

Instead, take your time on the passage. Focus on understanding precisely what the passage is saying. This approach might take you more time at first, but it is shocking how easy the questions are in RC when you have fully understood what the passage is saying.

Reading the Passage

In this section, I will present you with a reading comprehension passage. Read it using what you just learned. Then, we will go through it together.

PT19 Section 4 Passage 1

Wherever the crime novels of P. D. James are discussed by critics, there is a tendency on the one hand to exaggerate her merits and on the other to castigate her as a genre writer who is getting above herself. Perhaps underlying the debate is that familiar, false opposition set up between different kinds of fiction, according to which enjoyable novels are held to be somehow slightly lowbrow, and a novel is not considered true literature unless it is a tiny bit dull.

Those commentators who would elevate James's books to the status of high literature point to her painstakingly constructed characters, her elaborate settings, her sense of place, and her love of abstractions: notions about morality, duty, pain, and pleasure are never far from the lips of her police officers and murderers. Others find her pretentious and tiresome; an inverted snobbery accuses her of abandoning the time-honored conventions of the detective genre in favor of a highbrow literary style. The critic Harriet Waugh wants P. D. James to get on with "the more taxing business of laying a tricky trail and then fooling the reader"; Philip Oakes in The Literary Review groans, "Could we please proceed with the business of clapping the handcuffs on the killer?"

James is certainly capable of strikingly good writing. She takes immense trouble to provide her characters with convincing histories and passions. Her descriptive digressions are part of the pleasure of her books and give them dignity and weight. But it is equally true that they frequently interfere with the story; the patinas and aromas of a country kitchen receive more loving attention than does the plot itself. Her devices to advance the story can be shameless and thin, and it is often impossible to see how her detectives arrive at the truth; one is left to conclude that the detectives solve crimes through intuition. At this stage in her career P. D. James seems to be less interested in the specifics of detection than in her characters' vulnerabilities and perplexities.

However, once the rules of a chosen genre camp creative thought, there is no reason why an able and interesting writer should accept them. In her latest book, there are signs that James is beginning to feel constrained by the crime-novel genre. Here, her determination to leave areas of ambiguity in the solution of the crime and to distribute guilt among the murderer, victim, and bystanders points to a conscious rebellion against the traditional neatness of detective fiction. It is fashionable, though reprehensible, for one writer to prescribe to another. But perhaps the time has come for P. D. James to slide out of her handcuffs and stride into the territory of the mainstream novel.

After reading this passage, you should have a pretty good idea about what we are talking about.

What was this passage about? You should be able to tell me. After reading it yourself, write down what you thought the main point was.

Alright, let's go through this passage together.

"Wherever the crime novels of P. D. James are discussed by critics, there is a tendency on the one hand to exaggerate her merits and on the other to castigate her as a genre writer who is getting above herself."

The passage tells us about this crime novelist P. D. James, and it also tells us that when critical circles discuss her, there are two tendencies. One camp of critics thinks P. D. James is excellent and exaggerates how good she is. On the other hand, some critics dismiss P. D. James and believe she should merely stick to crime novels. They call her a "genre writer." I interpreted this as an insult. They do not view P. D. James as an accomplished writer, and they think she should only stick in her lane of writing crime novels. Either way, we know that we have these two groups of critics. One that views P. D. James very fondly and one that thinks she is merely a genre writer. If you are not having a mental conversation like this with yourself, start doing so. You need to be reacting and comprehending as you read these passages.

"Perhaps underlying the debate is that familiar, false opposition set up between different kinds of fiction, according to which enjoyable novels are held to be somehow slightly lowbrow, and a novel is not considered true literature unless it is a tiny bit dull."

Now the passage gives us a possible reason for this dichotomy. The passage tells us that in the past, novels viewed as enjoyable are not truly high literature. For something to be high literature, it must be at least somewhat dull. Perhaps this is why Harry Potter, widely viewed as engaging literature, is not considered as great of literature as Charles Dickens. Many people think Harry Potter is more entertaining than Dickens. Still, if it is true that great literature must be somewhat dull, that would explain why Dickens is classified as great while Harry Potter is not.

This would explain why the hostile critics think James is a genre writer. Perhaps her writing is not dull and does not meet one of the required conditions for her literature to be great. It would also explain those that overly praise her. I'm now picturing this group of critics as fans that love James's work. This is a possible explanation for why we have these two separate groups.

"Those commentators who would elevate James's books to the status of high literature point to her painstakingly constructed characters, her elaborate settings, her sense of place, and her love of abstractions: notions about morality, duty, pain, and pleasure are never far from the lips of her police officers and murderers."

The passage discusses one of the two groups of critics we have identified. We are specifically looking at the critics that like James's works. The passage gives reasons for why they view her work as high literature. They tell us that she uses elaborate settings, has complex notions about morality, etc. I expect them to talk about the other group of critics and why they don't like James's work. I could be wrong about where I expect them to go, but by having a prediction, we are reassuring ourselves that we are engaged with the passage.

"Others find her pretentious and tiresome; an inverted snobbery accuses her of abandoning the time-honored conventions of the detective genre in favor of a highbrow literary style."

The passage met my prediction. We do turn towards the other group of critics. These critics are the ones that do not like James's works. The passage says that she is pretentious and tiresome. It also says that she is abandoning past conventions of detective novels and is doing her own new literary style, which the passage describes as highbrow.

"The critic Harriet Waugh wants P. D. James to get on with "the more taxing business of laying a tricky trail and then fooling the reader"; Philip Oakes in The Literary Review groans, "Could we please proceed with the business of clapping the handcuffs on the killer?"

The passage now cites specific critics who dislike James's works. Waugh points out that James is taking too long to get into the details of the mystery. Oakes echoes this critique and agrees that James is not spending enough time on the actual crime.

"James is certainly capable of strikingly good writing."

This sentence feels like a conclusion, so we should quickly note that this is what our author thinks. We don't need to write this down, but it's worthwhile to make a mental note here that our author believes that James is capable of good writing.

"She takes immense trouble to provide her characters with convincing histories and passions."

Now the author gives reasons why they think James is capable of good writing. The author cites how James gives her characters good backgrounds.

"Her descriptive digressions are part of the pleasure of her books and give them dignity and weight."

Our author continues to hammer home the idea that James's writing is strengthened by her descriptions of the characters. It is worth noting that "descriptive digressions" could refer to more than just the characters. It could include the setting, for example.

"But it is equally true that they frequently interfere with the story; the patinas and aromas of a country kitchen receive more loving attention than does the plot itself."

Our author now concedes that there is some truth to the criticisms made towards James. James sometimes does spend too much time describing things and not enough time on the plot. Our author seems to fall in between our two groups of critics.

"Her devices to advance the story can be shameless and thin, and it is often impossible to see how her detectives arrive at the truth; one is left to conclude that the detectives solve crimes through intuition."

The passage discusses how James focuses less on the plot and more on describing things. This would appear to be a problem for crime novels. To my understanding, part of the appeal of a crime novel is to leave a trail of cues. When the crime is solved, the reader understands how all the pieces fit together. James is disregarding this, according to our author.

"At this stage in her career P. D. James seems to be less interested in the specifics of detection than in her characters' vulnerabilities and perplexities."

Our author supports the idea that P. D. James is more focused on the characters than she is in the detective aspect of things. Once again, this supports the idea that James is neglecting the standard conventions of crime novels. At this point, I view James as someone who feels trapped by the traditions of crime novels and wants to expand beyond the genre in which she first had success.

"However, once the rules of a chosen genre camp creative thought, there is no reason why an able and interesting writer should accept them."

Here, the passage again gives a statement that reads like a conclusion. The fact that it reads as a conclusion tells us that our author is giving their opinion. Our author says that James does not have to stay within the confines of her genre. Even though these conventional standards do exist, James does not have to stick to them, according to our author.

"In her latest book, there are signs that James is beginning to feel constrained by the crime-novel genre."

We now know that James is starting to explore away from her genre of crime. The passage had already told us this was happening, but this sentence makes it a little more explicit.

"Here, her determination to leave areas of ambiguity in the solution of the crime and to distribute guilt among the murderer, victim, and bystanders points to a conscious rebellion against the traditional neatness of detective fiction."

The passage tells us how James is branching off traditional crime-novel norms. The passage cites her distributing guilt to multiple people as one way she breaks norms.

"It is fashionable, though reprehensible, for one writer to prescribe to another."

Our author once again is speaking their mind. They say that writers should not tell one another how to write, even though it may be prevalent in their circles.

"But perhaps the time has come for P. D. James to slide out of her handcuffs and stride into the territory of the mainstream novel."

The final sentence of the passage once again reveals what our author thinks. Our author believes P. D. James has reached her potential with crime novels and should turn to the more mainstream novel.

At this point, we understand everything about this passage. Just by reading it, we've identified every part of the passage. We know about the two critic groups and why they like/dislike James's work. We also know how our author feels about James's work.

We can now confidently move into the questions.

Question 1

Which of the following best states the author's main conclusion?

On RC, we want to be predicting the answers. We already know what our author's main conclusion was. Reading the answers will result in us getting bogged down by their ideas. We want to predict before we move into the answers.

Let's remind ourselves what the author's main conclusion was. Take a moment to think for yourself.

The author's main conclusion was that P. D. James is ready to branch out from the traditional confines of the crime novel. We can look at the answers now that we've predicted our answer.

A. Because P. D. James's potential as a writer is stifled by her chosen genre, she should turn her talents towards writing mainstream novels.

B. Because the requirements of the popular novel are incompatible with true creative expression, P. D. James's promise as a serious author has been diminished.

C. The dichotomy between popular and sophisticated literature is well illustrated in the crime novels of P. D. James.

D. The critics who have condemned P. D. James's lack of attention to the specifics of detection fail to take into account her carefully constructed plots.

E. Although her plots are not always neatly resolved, the beauty of her descriptive passages justifies P. D. James's decision to write in the crime-novel genre.

Which of these best matches our prediction?

A fits our prediction amazingly! The passage says that the crime-novel genre has too limited P. D. James, so it is time for her to branch out.

B is wrong because the passage doesn't discuss how James's promise has been diminished. The passage still thinks she is promising. She just needs to branch out to other genres.

C is wrong because there is no dichotomy within James's work.

D is wrong because the passage doesn't focus on this. The passage briefly mentions both sides of critics to line up our argument about how James should evolve as a writer, but this is not the focal point of the passage. D is too narrow.

E is wrong because it is the opposite of what the passage is talking about. Our passage concedes that James is branching out from the traditions of the crime novel. E flat-out misdescribes what is going on.

Question 2

The author refers to the "patinas and aromas of a country kitchen" (middle of the third paragraph) most probably in order to

Let's go back to our passage to get the context of what the passage was saying with this quote.

James is certainly capable of strikingly good writing. She takes immense trouble to provide her characters with convincing histories and passions. Her descriptive digressions are part of the pleasure of her books and give them dignity and weight. But it is equally true that they frequently interfere with the story; the **patinas and aromas of a country kitchen** *receive more loving attention than does the plot itself.*

Ask yourself why the author brings up this example of "patinas and aromas."

The author mentions "patinas and aromas" as an example to support the idea that James is overly focused on describing things.

Now that we know why the author used this quote let's look at our answers.

    A. Illustrate James's gift for innovative phrasing
    B. Highlight James's interest in rural society
    C. Allow the reader to experience the pleasure of James's books
    D. Explain how James typically constructs her plot
    E. Exemplify James's preoccupation with descriptive writing.

A is wrong because the point here is not to say that James used big words.

B is wrong because the point had nothing to do with saying James focused on rural societies.

C is wrong because it has nothing to do with the pleasure of reading James's books.

D is wrong because it has nothing to do with plots.

E is correct because it describes what the author was doing here. The author gave an example of how James overly focuses on describing things.

In RC, the wrong answers can be terrible. Knowing what you are looking for before you go into these answers allows you to reject the wrong ones quickly.

Question 3

The second paragraph serves primarily to

The question is simply asking us what the second paragraph is doing. Let's look back at our second paragraph to remind ourselves.

Those commentators who would elevate James's books to the status of high literature point to her painstakingly constructed characters, her elaborate settings, her sense of place, and her love of abstractions: notions about morality, duty, pain, and pleasure are never far from the lips of her police officers and murderers. Others find her pretentious and tiresome; an inverted snobbery accuses her of abandoning the time-honored conventions of the detective genre in favor of a highbrow literary style. The critic Harriet Waugh wants P. D. James to get on with "the more taxing business of laying a tricky trail and then fooling the reader"; Philip Oakes in The Literary Review groans, "Could we please proceed with the business of clapping the handcuffs on the killer?"

In this paragraph, the passage expands upon the two groups of critics mentioned in the first paragraph. It explains why one group of critics like James and explains why the other group does not like James.

Put simply, the second paragraph expands upon the two groups of critics the passage mentions in the first paragraph. Let's check our answers now.

    A. Propose an alternative to two extreme opinions described earlier
    B. Present previously mentioned positions in greater detail
    C. Contradict an assertion cited previously
    D. Introduce a controversial interpretation
    E. Analyze a dilemma in greater depth

One of these matches our prediction, and four do not. Take a second to identify the correct answer.

A is wrong because there is no alternative in this paragraph. Later in the passage, our author gives their perspective, which is milder than the previous opinions. However, this does not happen in our second paragraph.

B is correct because it describes what the second paragraph is doing. This paragraph tells us more about the two groups of critics.

C is wrong because there is no contradiction of an assertion. This paragraph describes two positions.

D is wrong because this paragraph does not introduce any new position. It just expands upon previously mentioned ones.

E is wrong because there is no dilemma.

Question 4

The passage supports which one of the following statements about detective fiction?

This is an open-ended question, so it isn't easy to predict. Instead, we need to read each answer and ask ourselves if we discussed it. We need an answer that we can directly support with the text.

The one thing I do remember is that crime novels typically follow certain conventions. This idea was brought up to contrast how James differs from her genre.

Here are the answers.

   A. There are as many different detective-novel conventions as there are writers of crime novels.
   B. Detective fiction has been characterized by extremely high literary quality.
   C. Detective fiction has been largely ignored by literary critics.
   D. There is very little agreement among critics about the basic elements of a typical detective novel.
   E. Writers of detective fiction have customarily followed certain conventions in constructing their novels.

You can quickly read them to see if any of these ring a bell. Only one will be supportable, so if you can prove one, it will be the answer. If none sound familiar, you can go through them one by one.

A says, "There are as many different detective-novel conventions as there are writers of crime novels." This is misdescribing what the passage said. The passage said there is one set of conventions, not multiple. A is wrong.

B says, "Detective fiction has been characterized by extremely high literary quality." The passage never says whether or not detective fiction is of high or low literary quality, so we cannot pick this answer. B is wrong.

C says, "Detective fiction has been largely ignored by literary critics." The passage does not talk about this. All we know is that some critics are at least talking about P. D. James's work. We have no idea if detective fiction is being ignored more broadly. We cannot support this answer, so C is wrong.

D says, "There is very little agreement among critics about the basic elements of a typical detective novel." This is similar to A and says that there are no standard conventions for detective novels. We know that there are standard conventions, so D is wrong.

E says, "Writers of detective fiction have customarily followed certain conventions in constructing their novels." Perfect. We know this is true. This quote from the passage, "an inverted snobbery accuses her of abandoning the time-honored conventions of the detective genre in favor of a highbrow literary style," directly supports this answer.

Question 5

The passage suggests that both Waugh and Oakes consider James's novels to have

What do we know about Waugh and Oakes? You should remember that these are two of the critics that do not like James's works. Let's look back at the paragraph where we mention them.

Others find her pretentious and tiresome; an inverted snobbery accuses her of abandoning the time-honored conventions of the detective genre in favor of a highbrow literary style. The critic Harriet Waugh wants P. D. James to get on with "the more taxing business of laying a tricky trail and then fooling the reader"; Philip Oakes in The Literary Review groans, "Could we please proceed with the business of clapping the handcuffs on the killer?"

You should see that Waugh and Oakes think James spends too much time describing things and not enough time on the crime.

Our prediction here should be that Waugh and Oakes consider James's novels to lack details relevant to the crime and to have too many details irrelevant to the crime.

Now let's check our answers.

A. Too much material that is extraneous to the solution of the crime
B. Too little characterization to enable the reader to solve the crime
C. Too few suspects to generate suspense
D. Too simple a plot to hold the attention of the reader
E. Too convoluted a plot for the reader to understand

A is good and matches our prediction. Both Waugh and Oakes talk about how James spends too much time on irrelevant information.

B is wrong because Waugh and Oakes don't talk about characterization.

C is wrong because Waugh and Oakes don't mention the number of suspects.

D is wrong because Waugh and Oakes are not criticizing James based on her plot complexity.

E is wrong because Waugh and Oakes are not criticizing James based on her plot complexity.

Question 6

It can be inferred from the passage that, in the author's view, traditional detective fiction is characterized by

Once again, we have a relatively open-ended question. One thing to note here is that the LSAT asks us "what can be inferred." This phrasing sometimes trips people up. The LSAT does not want us to "infer" but instead wants us to repeat something the author talked about. Quickly ask yourself what the author said about traditional detective fiction.

All I explicitly remember here is that traditional detective fiction has certain conventions. I also remember that we say there is typically only one person to blame. One of these might be the answer, but it's hard to know with open-ended questions. At this point, we can move into the answers.

- A. Concern for the weaknesses and doubts of the characters
- B. Transparent devices to advance the plot
- C. The attribution of intuition to the detective
- D. The straightforward assignment of culpability for the crime
- E. Attention to the concepts of morality and responsibility

A says, "Concern for the weaknesses and doubts of the characters." P. D. James seems to care about this, but the passage never says that is typical of crime novels. A is wrong.

B says, "Transparent devices to advance the plot." The passage never says that crime novels typically have transparent devices. The passage attributes this to P. D. James, so B misdescribes the passage. B is wrong.

C says, "The attribution of intuition to the detective." Once again, this is said about P. D. James, but the passage never says this about crime novels in general.

D says, "The straightforward assignment of culpability for the crime."
The passage does refer to this when it says, "Here, her determination to
leave areas of ambiguity in the solution of the crime and to distribute
guilt among the murderer, victim, and bystanders points to a conscious
rebellion against the traditional neatness of detective fiction." This
excerpt directly supports D as our answer.

E says, "Attention to the concepts of morality and responsibility." Once
again, this is something P. D. James says, but it is not something that is
attributed as a convention of crime novels.

Question 7

The author characterizes the position of some critics as "inverted snobbery" (middle of the second paragraph) because they hold which one of the following views?

This question asks us why the author used the phrase "inverted snobbery." At this point, we want to look at the paragraph to see the context. One thing to note is the use of "they" in the question. "They" refers to the last noun mentioned in the sentence. Here, that noun would be the critics. They are asking us what positions the critics hold, not the position our author holds. You need to understand this pronoun rule. This will show up on the LSAT, so understand what "they" is referring to. As you'll see, the LSAT even has trap answers for people that do not discern this difference.

Those commentators who would elevate James's books to the status of high literature point to her painstakingly constructed characters, her elaborate settings, her sense of place, and her love of abstractions: notions about morality, duty, pain, and pleasure are never far from the lips of her police officers and murderers. Others find her pretentious and tiresome; an **inverted snobbery** accuses her of abandoning the time-honored conventions of the detective genre in favor of a highbrow literary style. The critic Harriet Waugh wants P. D. James to get on with "the more taxing business of laying a tricky trail and then fooling the reader"; Philip Oakes in The Literary Review groans, "Could we please proceed with the business of clapping the handcuffs on the killer?"

What views do these critics hold?

These are the critics that do not like P. D. James. They think she should stick within the confines of her genre. They want her to spend more time on the plot and less describing things.

We have our prediction, so we can read the answers.

A. Critics of literature must acknowledge that they are less talented than creators of literature.
B. Critics should hesitate to disparage popular authors.
C. P. D. James's novels should focus less on characters from the English landed gentry.
D. Detective fiction should be content to remain an unambitious literary genre.
E. P. D. James should be less fastidious about portraying violence.

Several of these answers refer to what the author might think. They are preying on people that did not understand what "they" was referring back to in the question. We know that "they" refers to our critics, so we need to find the answer that describes what our critics think.

A is wrong because we are not talking about what people think about the critics. Instead, we want an answer that refers to what these critics think. This answer is trapping people that misunderstood the use of "they."

B is wrong for the same reason as A. We care what these critics think, not what to think of them.

C is wrong because we never talk about the English landed gentry. We cannot pick answers that are not supported by the passage.

D is correct because this matches what we know about these critics. We know these critics think that P. D. James is trying to do too much. Our critics think James should stick within the confines of detective fiction.

E is wrong because we never talk about James portraying violence.

Question 8

Which one of the following quotations about literature best exemplifies the "familiar" attitude mentioned in the second sentence of the passage?

Here, we need to figure out what this "familiar" attitude is. Once we know that, we can check each quotation they give us in the answers to see if the "familiar" attitude fits. Let's look back at the passage.

Wherever the crime novels of P. D. James are discussed by critics, there is a tendency on the one hand to exaggerate her merits and on the other to castigate her as a genre writer who is getting above herself. Perhaps underlying the debate is that **familiar**, false opposition set up between different kinds of fiction, according to which enjoyable novels are held to be somehow slightly lowbrow, and a novel is not considered true literature unless it is a tiny bit dull.

What does "familiar" mean here? In the same sentence, they say there is a false opposition between different kinds of fiction. The passage also says that for a novel to be high literature, it must be somewhat dull. Enjoyable novels cannot be high literature.

We now know what the "familiar" attitude refers to, so we can move into the answers and see which one fits.

- A. "The fantasy and whimsy characteristics of this writer's novels qualify them as truly great works of literature."
- B. "The greatest work of early English literature happens to be a highly humorous collection of tales."
- C. "A truly great work of literature should place demands upon its readers, rather than divert them."
- D. "Although many critics are condescending about best-selling novels, I would not wish to challenge the opinions of millions of readers."

E. "A novel need only satisfy the requirements of its particular genre to be considered a true work of literature."

We already know what our attitude is, so we can just read each answer and see if it fits.

A is wrong because our attitude seems to think that enjoyable novels are not great works of literature. A runs counter to our attitude.

B is wrong for the same reason as A. Enjoyable works are not great works of literature according to this attitude.

C is exactly what we are looking for. This attitude thinks that great works of literature are dull and hence place demands upon their readers.

D is wrong because we are not talking about judging the opinions of readers with this attitude.

E is wrong because we do not say that any novel that fulfills the expectations of its genre is a great work of literature.

Closing Thoughts

Reading comprehension requires you to read closely and parrot back at the LSAT what the passage has just told you. It requires practice, but the questions are easy if you commit to understanding the passage.

The correct answers are directly supported by the passage. To pick an answer, you should be able to cite lines of the passage that support it.

The questions we did together should have felt easy. Read the passages closely, and they will feel this way on the test.

Logic Games

Logic Games

In this section, we are going to go through logic games. Logic games are often people's worst section when they initially approach the LSAT. Still, it is the most learnable section of the test. Many people never miss a logic games question. You can get there, too, if you put in the proper practice.

Logic games requires work. To do well on these, you will need to grind it out. Once you do enough, LG gets to be the most straightforward section of the test.

First, we are going to cover basic LG concepts. After we cover those, we will apply these concepts to an actual logic game.

Logic Games Basics

We will go through a game and all of its questions shortly. However, before we do that, I wanted to quickly run through some LG concepts.

Game Types

There are several kinds of games that you will see repeatedly on the LSAT. Often, the LSAT will ask you to put variables in order. For example, it may ask you to order seven runners in a race.

Another typical game you will have is grouping. You may have nine students and have to assign them to three groups.

There is no need to study these game types. While you will see certain setups over and over, all of the games test your ability to understand how various rules interact. The real problem with learning game types is that the LSAT loves to throw curveballs. There will be games that are entirely of their own kind. Learning to solve logic games by game type falls apart for these games because they are different.

These anomalous games are often the easiest if you can set them up properly. The approach you will learn in this section is to make inferences and set up a game board regardless of what the test throws at you.

Do the Work Upfront

In logic games, the LSAT will give you a paragraph describing a scenario. This scenario will involve assigning variables in some way.

The key to LG is to create a diagram that allows you to view the rules as you work through the questions. After you've initially read the rules and the scenario, you should create a diagram. This diagram should visualize all of the rules on the page. Then, solving the questions often becomes easy. The key is that you must include all of the relevant information.

With a good diagram, the questions on LG are easy.

Diagramming Basics

There is no single correct way to diagram rules on the LSAT. I have my personal preference, and you will develop your own through your study. You are welcome to plagiarize mine, but you can also adjust things yourself.

For example, if a rule says that Johnny and Lauren cannot be in the same group for a field trip, I might diagram that like this.

J/L

That may or may not make sense to you. Figure out a way to put rules on the page that you understand. They may also say that Johnny and Harrison have to be together. I might diagram that like this.

J+H

You need to figure out a system that works for you. The important thing is that you can get all the information from the scenario and the rules onto the page.

High Level of Proof

On LG, we prove our answers. If I were to ask you what 2+2 is, you know with 100% confidence what the answer is. If I had you bet your life on it, you would feel pretty comfortable because you know that 2+2=4. There is no doubt in your mind.

That confidence is the confidence you should have when picking answers in LG. These questions are 100% solvable, just like simple math questions. You need to be confident in the answer you are choosing. Picking an LG answer choice without this level of confidence means you didn't even do the question. Anything short of solving these questions is unacceptable in this section.

Setting up the Diagram

The first step on LG is to read the setup for the game. Read the paragraph first to understand what you are trying to do.

PT19 Section 1 Game 1

During a period of six consecutive days—day 1 through day 6—each of exactly six factories—F, G, H, J, Q, and R—will be inspected. During this period, each of the factories will be inspected exactly one, one factory per day. The schedule for the inspections must conform to the following conditions:

    F is inspected on either day 1 or day 6.

    J is inspected on an earlier day than Q is inspected.

    Q is inspected on the day immediately before R is inspected.

    If G is inspected on day 3, Q is inspected on day 5.

What are they asking us to do here? They want us to order these six factory inspections from 1-6. The beginning of our diagram should look something like this:

___   ___   ___   ___   ___   ___

Here, each line represents a day. Now we have to fill in the slots with factories. First, we need to add our rules to the diagram.

The first rule is "F is inspected on either day 1 or day 6." Diagramming is a personal preference, which you can approach in a few ways. I would put it on the right side of my page like this.

— — — — — —   F = 1 or 6

You can add it to the actual diagram, if that makes more sense to you, like this.

— — — — — —
F̶ F̶ F̶ F̶   F = 1 or 6

Here, the Fs with slashes show that these are not slots F can go. This incorporates our rules that F must be on day one or day six into our diagram.

Our second rule is "J is inspected on an earlier day than Q is inspected." I would add this to the side like this.

— — — — — —
F̶ F̶ F̶ F̶   F = 1 or 6
                                                     J→Q

Here, we can see that J has to come before Q. We also know that since J has to go before Q, it can never be the last day inspected. Q can also never be the first day inspected. We can add this to our diagram.

— — — — — —
Q̶ F̶ F̶ F̶ F̶ J̶   F = 1 or 6
                                                     J→Q

The third rule is "Q is inspected on the day immediately before R is inspected." We already have a rule about where Q must go, so I would incorporate this rule into that rule.

| — | — | — | — | — | — |

Q̶ F̶ F̶ F̶ F̶ J̶   F =1 or 6

                                                          J→QR

We now have our rules that R has to come right after Q in our rules. By combining these rules, we can see that J has to go before both Q and R. We can also figure out that J cannot go fifth because it has to come before at least two more inspections. We can also figure out that the earliest R can come is third because we need at least two inspections before it. We can add these to our diagram as well.

| — | — | — | — | — | — |

Q̶ F̶ F̶ F̶ F̶ J̶   F =1 or 6

R̶ R̶   J̶   J→QR

Our final rule is "If G is inspected on day 3, Q is inspected on day 5." I would write this rule to the side like this.

| — | — | — | — | — | — |

Q̶ F̶ F̶ F̶ F̶ J̶   F =1 or 6

R̶ R̶   J̶   J→QR

                                                          If G=3, Q=5

Now that we finished diagramming, we want to quickly ask ourselves if any variables have no constraints. H has no constraints. This is called a floater. H is not constrained and can do many things in our game. H still has to abide by the constraints that affect the rest of the variables, but H itself can go wherever.

Now that we have our diagram and understand what is going on, we can move into the questions.

Question 1

Which one of the following could be a list of the factories in the order of their scheduled inspections, from day 1 through day 6?

This is often the first question for a game. They are going to give us five orders of our factories. We have to figure out which one is in an allowable order. You can solve these questions using the process of elimination.

The answers are:

    A. F, Q, R, H, J, G
    B. G, H, J, Q, R, F
    C. G, J, Q, H, R, F
    D. G, J, Q, R, F, H
    E. J, H, G, Q, R, F

With these questions, look at each rule we have. Take that rule and see if the answers follow it. If the answer does not follow the rule, we can get rid of that answer.

Our first rule is that F must be 1st or 6th. Check the answers to make sure they are following that rule. We can get rid of any answers that violate that rule.

You should notice that all of the answers follow this rule except for D. We can get rid of D and move on to our next rule.

    A. F, Q, R, H, J, G
    B. G, H, J, Q, R, F
    C. G, J, Q, H, R, F
    D. ~~G, J, Q, R, F, H~~
    E. J, H, G, Q, R, F

Our second rule is that J has to come before Q. We combined this with our third rule that Q has to go immediately before R. Check the answers to ensure they conform to the J→QR rule.

You should notice that a few answers violate this rule. A has J after Q, and R. C has Q and R not adjacent to each other. We can cross these answers off and move on to our next rule.

A. ~~F, Q, R, H, J, G~~
B. G, H, J, Q, R, F
C. ~~G, J, Q, H, R, F~~
D. ~~G, J, Q, R, F, H~~
E. J, H, G, Q, R, F

We have one rule left and two answers. We now need to ensure that when G is 3rd, Q is 5th. We can see that this only applies to one of our remaining scenarios, E. E has G 3rd but has Q 4th. This violates our rule. We can get rid of E. Only B remains, and we can pick B as our answer.

Question 2

Which one of the following must be false?

With an open-ended question like this, read the answers and ask yourself if it seems plausible knowing our diagram.

$\overline{\ }$	$\overline{\ }$	$\overline{\ }$	$\overline{\ }$	$\overline{\ }$	$\overline{\ }$
Q̶	F	F̶	F	F	J̶
R̶	R̶			J̶	

F =1 or 6

J→QR

If G=3, Q=5

    A. The inspection of G is scheduled for day 4.
    B. The inspection of H is scheduled for day 6.
    C. The inspection of J is scheduled for day 4.
    D. The inspection of Q is scheduled for day 3.
    E. The inspection of R is scheduled for day 2.

Look through these answers and ask yourself if any of them are invalid.

A through D seem possible, but it's hard to know without testing them out. However, E jumps out at me. We know that R can never be second on our diagram, so E is the answer.

We can also check this manually (don't do this on test day, I am just doing it to show you how we know R can never be second).

$\underline{\ \ }$ R $\underline{\ \ }$ $\underline{\ \ }$ $\underline{\ \ }$ $\underline{\ \ }$

We know that J→QR. R is in the second spot, so putting J and Q before it causes us to have a real problem. We only have one slot to put two variables. This is impossible and proves to us that E is the answer.

Question 3

The inspection for which one of the following CANNOT be scheduled for day 5?

Look at our diagram to see who cannot go on day 5. We know that both F and J can never be on day 5. Then check the answers to see if they give us either of these options.

```
—  —  —  —  —  —
Q̶  F̶  F̶  F̶  F̶  J̶
R̶  R̶       J̶
```

F = 1 or 6

J→QR

If G=3, Q=5

A. G
B. H
C. J
D. Q
E. R

They give us J. That is our answer. C is the answer.

Question 4

The inspections scheduled for day 3 and day 5, respectively, could be those of

This question's first step is eliminating any answers that violate our diagram. We know that F can never be third. We also know that F and J can never be fifth. Apply this to our answers first.

— — — — — —

Q̶ F̶ F̶ F̶ F̶ J̶   F = 1 or 6
R̶ R̶   J̶   J→QR
                                          If G=3, Q=5

    A. G and H
    B. G and R
    C. H and G
    D. R and J
    E. R and H

F being third is never an issue here. However, they have J fifth in D, so we can eliminate D.

    A. G and H
    B. G and R
    C. H and G
    D. R̶ ̶a̶n̶d̶ ̶J̶
    E. R and H

Let's look at A. In A, we have G third. What do we know about G being third? We know that when G is third, Q has to be 5th. A violates this. B has the same problem. We can get rid of A and B.

A. ~~G and H~~
B. ~~G and R~~
C. H and G
D. ~~R and J~~
E. R and H

Only C and E are left. Nothing jumps out at me, so at this point, I would test them to see which one works. Let's test C.

_ _ H _ G _

We have to assign J→QR to fulfill our rules. We cannot do this with H and G where they are. We can get rid of C.

Only E is left, so we can pick E as our answer.

I would not do this on test day, but we can make a scenario where E works. That scenario is JQRGHF.

Question 5

If the inspection of R is scheduled for the day immediately before the inspection of F, which one of the following must be true about the schedule?

Q ~~F~~ ~~F~~ ~~F~~ ~~F~~ ~~J~~
~~R~~ ~~R~~   ~~J~~

F = 1 or 6

J→QRF

If G=3, Q=5

In this question, they give us a new rule. We now know that R comes immediately before F. We can add this to our J→QR rule to create J→QRF. We also know that F has to be either first or sixth. We know that F cannot be first because it must come after R, so we know F has to be sixth. We also know that Q and R must be fourth and fifth, respectively, to fulfill our rules.

Our situation looks like this:

_ _ _ Q R F

Let's check out answers to see if they give us "Q must be fourth."

    A. The inspection of either G or H is scheduled for day 1.
    B. The inspection of either G or J is scheduled for day 1.
    C. The inspection of either G or J is scheduled for day 2.
    D. The inspection of either H or J is scheduled for day 3.
    E. The inspection of either H or J is scheduled for day 4.

None of these jump out to me as the correct answer. We know that E is incorrect because we have already assigned Q to day 4, but beyond that,

A-D all have to do with assigning G, H, and J. At this point, ask yourself what you know about each variable.

We know H is a floater and does not have limitations. We also know the only rule J has to conform to is that it comes before Q and R.

We also know that if G is third, Q has to be fifth. Q is not fifth in our scenario; hence, G can never be third. This means that either H or J has to be third.

This is D. We know this must be true, so we can pick D.

Question 6

If the inspections of G and H are scheduled, not necessarily in that order, for days as far apart as possible, which one of the following is a complete and accurate list of the factories any of which could be scheduled for inspection for day 1?

This question is wordy, so make sure you understand what the question is asking you. The question asks us to put G and H as far apart as possible. However, the question is, given that we meet that condition, what factories can be inspected on day 1? The first step is to figure out how far apart G and H can be from one another.

— — — — — —

Q̶ F̶ F̶ F̶ F̶ J̶   F =1 or 6
R̶ R̶   J̶   J→QR
                    If G=3, Q=5

We know that F has to be either 1 or 6, so we cannot put G and H on opposite ends of the diagram. At this point, make a possible setup where we have them as far apart as possible. We are testing to see if we can make them four spots away from one another.

F G J Q R H

That worked, so we know we must have them four spots away from one another. Now let's look at the answers to figure out how to approach these answers.

A. F, J
B. G, H
C. G, H, J

D. F, G, H
E. F, G, H, J

We already know from our test setup that F can be first, so we can eliminate B and C.

A. F, J
B. ~~G, H~~
C. ~~G, H, J~~
D. F, G, H
E. F, G, H, J

At this point, we want to figure out which variables are worth testing. I would test J next.

J _ _ _ _ F

Putting J first is going to cause real problems for us. We know that F has to be first or sixth, so F has to go sixth. This cannot work for us because we need G and H to be four spots away from each other. Now, the maximum distance they can be is three spots. Based on this, we can get rid of J as a possibility for day 1.

This removes A and E. Only D is left, so we can pick D as our answer.

Question 7

If the inspection of G is scheduled for the day immediately before the inspection of Q, which one of the following could be true?

This question is modifying a rule. We can change our J→QR rule to be J→GQR. Now with a could be true question, we just need to prove one of the answers. It's open-ended, so we can read the answers and ask ourselves if it seems possible.

$\overline{Q}$ $\overline{F}$ $\overline{F}$ $\overline{F}$ $\overline{F}$ $\overline{J}$

Q F F F F J
R R   J

F = 1 or 6
J→QR
If G=3, Q=5

A. The inspection of G is scheduled for day 5.
B. The inspection of H is scheduled for day 6.
C. The inspection of J is scheduled for day 2.
D. The inspection of Q is scheduled for day 4.
E. The inspection of R is scheduled for day 3.

I would go through these one by one.

A does not work because G cannot go fifth with our new rule. If G were fifth, we would need to put Q and R after it. There is only one slot for two variables; hence, G cannot be fifth.

B seems plausible. Let's test it.

F J G Q R H

With H being sixth, we know that F has to be first. This forces JGQR into the middle four spots. Here, we run into trouble. When we do this, we have G third. We know that when G is third, Q has to be fifth, but our setup does not permit this. B is wrong.

C also seems plausible. Let's test it.

F J H G Q R

We can make a setup that works with J being second. Since this is a could be true, we've met our burden of proof, and we can pick C.

D cannot work because when we put Q fourth, we must put G and R next to it like this.

_ _ G Q R _

This activates our rule that when G is third, Q must be fifth. However, Q is fourth here so our rule is broken. Thus, this is an invalid setup.

E cannot work because we need J, G, and Q to all come before R. If R is on day 3, there are only two slots for three variables to go. This is a real problem for us and makes E incorrect.

Closing Thoughts

Logic games are solvable. If you embrace this high burden of proof, you will do well. Your ability to move through the games with speed will come as you do more of them. You need to make sure that you are solving these games. The people who do not improve on LG try to rush and don't solve the questions. If you are missing LG questions that you are attempting, you are not studying correctly. Occasionally, you'll misread something. This should be rare. If you regularly miss several of the questions you are attempting, you are not doing LG the right way.

LG also requires work. It may take you hundreds of games to get to perfect games. It will not take that long for most of you, but if you are serious about a legal career, you need to be willing to grind these out.

I wouldn't want a lawyer who quit after only 25 games.

Closing Thoughts

Other Thoughts

At this point, you should understand that the LSAT is a learnable test. If you are willing to put the work in, you can succeed and get a high score. In this section, I want to cover some non-LSAT question-related tips so that your study is efficient.

You Must Understand This Test

We've gone through about thirty actual LSAT questions at this point. You likely understood all of them. The LSAT is understandable. You are capable of figuring these questions out. If you want to score high, there are no gimmicks that will get you there. You must understand what is going on to score a high LSAT score.

This approach is the easy way, and it gets the highest scores. Focus on understanding each question and answer. You will do excellent. It will take repetition to drill things in, but if you focus on understanding what is on the page, the sky is the limit.

Pacing

Rushing on the LSAT is one of the most common mistakes new LSAT preppers make. By rushing, these good-intentioned takers allow themselves to not truly do questions to the proper burden of proof.

I don't want you worrying about timing. When you start an LSAT section, you only have one job. Get the next question right. I don't care if it takes you 30 seconds or 5 minutes. I do not want you to move on from that question until you are confident you are getting it right.

You may start by only attempting two games or 12 LR questions. However, you must recognize that this is a starting point and that you will get deeper in the section as you improve on the test. Speed comes with understanding.

If you try to rush through the section to finish and then build understanding, you will never get to perfection. You will be allowing yourself to be lazy and miss questions as you rush in the name of finishing the test. This does not work. Focus on your accuracy, and your speed will come.

Do the Work Upfront

The LSAT is much easier when you do the work upfront.

On LR, you need to comprehend the argument. Take the time to understand what they are saying, come up with an objection, and then fly through the answers. Good LSAT takers spend time on the passage and less time on the answers. This is because they already know what they are looking for.

On RC, understand what the passage is saying. If you do this, many of the answers are obviously incorrect. If you don't understand the passage, these questions are incredibly difficult. However, if you do, they are pretty straightforward.

On LG, making a good diagram is necessary. If you don't have all the rules condensed in a way you can understand, it will be hard to move through the questions.

Do the work upfront, and when you get to the answers, you can quickly identify what you are looking for.

Skipping Questions?

In short, you really should not be skipping questions.

In LR, never skip. Work from question 1 to the back of the section in order. LR has scaling difficulty, so the first questions are much easier than the last questions. They are all worth the same amount in your score, so I do not want you to skip question 4 to do question 25. Question 25 will almost certainly be much more complicated. As we've talked about, you don't have to finish.

In LG, you also should not skip. The games tend to be in progressive difficulty, so you should do them in order.

RC is a little different. The passages are not in any order of difficulty, so I do not care what order you do them in. However, I do not want you to spend time comparing passages. If you are going to do them out of order, pick a passage within a few seconds and begin. Don't quit and go back to another passage once you've started. Once you've selected a passage, you need to finish it. Do all the questions.

However, I would do all of the RC passages in order to keep it simple.

Be a Lawyer

The LSAT is your next step in your legal career. You need to take this seriously. When a lawyer gets an assignment at their firm, they do not half-ass it. Bring the same approach to the LSAT. You need to refuse to quit on this test.

You can figure this out. Lawyers figure this out. If you have what it takes to be a lawyer, you will do well on the LSAT.

Your LSAT score could be life-changing. A difference of 15 points can be the difference between being rejected from a school like Georgetown or attending on a full ride. Do not limit your future opportunities because you don't want to work hard on the LSAT.

Reading this book was an excellent first step. I'll leave you with a guide to self-study. After that, it's up to you. You control your outcome on this test. I hope for your sake you take it seriously.

Self Study Schedule

To learn the LSAT, you need to do the LSAT. Doing a section a day of the LSAT, under timed conditions, as we have discussed, will allow you to make consistent progress. Every day you take a section, the LSAT will tell you what you don't understand through the questions you miss. Through a thorough review of your mistakes, you will plug your holes. You will understand what mistakes you are making. If you do this enough, you will eventually fill nearly all your gaps.

This is the rough schedule I recommend.

Monday: LR section
Tuesday: RC section
Wednesday: LG section
Thursday: Weakest section
Friday: LR section
Saturday: Take a timed PT (three sections)
Sunday: Rest

You are welcome to modify this schedule to fit your life but do so with caution. I do not want you to cram all of these days into the weekend. Consistency on the LSAT goes a long way. This study schedule only takes about an hour a day, so you should be able to make time.

You can access most of the released LSATs by signing up for LSAC's Lawhub Prep Plus. It is $99 a year and is a must-have for LSAT prep. This will give you access to 74 old LSATs.

When you do a section, take it timed. As we've talked about, don't worry about finishing. Instead, focus on getting the question in front of you correct. I don't care how long it takes you. I care if you are getting the questions correct you are attempting. Solve these questions, don't just attempt them.

After you've finished a section (or the timer has gone off), stop working and go through your answers. Review any question you attempted and got incorrect. Review any question you weren't 100% sure about. Figure out what misled you about the wrong answer and why you missed the correct answer. After this, you have made progress and can comfortably move on. You have to take this review process seriously. Don't just look at the correct answer and tell yourself that you get it now. Figure it out. Review is where you progress.

With this schedule, it's hard to say how fast each individual will progress. I've seen people complete the process in a month, and I've seen others take a year. I expect it will take 3-6 months for the average person to reach their potential. However, this requires consistent work. Don't take weeks or months off. Consistent study is the best way to approach the LSAT.

Work With Me (and a small request)

Guidance can help throughout your LSAT journey.

If you liked how I explained the LSAT, you can check out my website lsasimplified.com to see what I am currently offering for LSAT prep.

I offer tutoring and live courses over Zoom currently.

I am also always available to answer questions via my email ben@lsasimplified.com.

I hope this book was able to help you! If it did help you, leaving a review on Amazon would help point other test takers towards this book. I'm much smaller than the big test companies, so I don't have the marketing budget they do. If you found this approach refreshing, tell a friend. Even better, write a review. Reviews tell the whole world what you were able to get from this book.

I appreciate your support.

Alright, we've reached the end. Remember that to have success on the LSAT, all you have to do is understand the damn words on the page.

Good luck!

Need more help?
Email me!

I can help!

This process doesn't need to be hard! I am available to help you get your best LSAT score and best law school admissions offers. I love this stuff and know a lot about it, so reach out with any questions you have. You can reach me at **ben@lsasimplified.com**. You can also check out my current offerings at lsasimplified.com.

You can also find me on Instagram where I post about upcoming LSATs, general LSAT news, and tips regarding this process. I offer live courses over Zoom as well as private tutoring for anyone that wants to work with me face to face.

 LSA Simplified